Title:
Khamoshi:
Echoes of Silence and Data Science

Table of Contents:

Introduction:

Khamoshi: Echoes of Silence tells the story of two AI researchers, Aditi and Arjun, whose love story unfolds through their mutual passion for data science and the art of learning together. The narrative explores their journey from initial attraction to deep emotional connection, interspersed with periods of silence, misunderstandings, and personal growth. Their bond is tested and strengthened through daily interactions centered around data science, leading them to both professional and emotional maturity.

Outline

Part I: The Beginning

Chapter 1: The Meeting

- *Introduce Aditi and Arjun, both passionate AI researchers.*
- *Set the stage with their initial meeting at a data science conference.*
- *Establish their professional connection and mutual admiration.*
-

Chapter 2: Data Science and Love

- *Describe how their professional collaboration begins with a joint research project.*
- *Reveal their budding interest in each other through shared passion and intellectual chemistry.*

-

Chapter 3: The Spark of Romance

- *Their relationship starts to blossom as they work closely together.*
- *Aditi and Arjun begin to explore their feelings for each other.*
-

-

Part II: The Conflict

Chapter 4: Misunderstandings

- Aditi and Arjun face their first major misunderstanding related to their project deadlines.
- A period of silence and confusion ensues, creating emotional distance.

Chapter 5: The Silence

- Detailed account of the two-week period of no communication.

- *Internal struggles and personal reflections by both characters.*

Chapter 6: Breaking the Silence

- *They reconnect after the silence, leading to a deeper conversation about their feelings and future.*

Part III: The Learning Curve

Chapter 7: Data Science Deep Dive

- *Aditi and Arjun embark on a structured learning journey, tackling basic to advanced data science concepts together.*

- *Daily interactions and discussions on topics like machine learning algorithms, data wrangling, and model evaluation.*

Chapter 8: Daywise Love and Learning

- *For 75 days, they engage in daily data science topics with a unique blend of romance and education.*

- *Their learning sessions include:*
  - **Day 1-10:** *Basics of Data Science (Statistics, Probability, Data Cleaning)*
  - **Day 11-20:** *Introduction to Machine Learning (Supervised vs. Unsupervised Learning)*
  - **Day 21-30:** *Advanced Algorithms (Neural Networks, SVM, Decision Trees)*
  - **Day 31-40:** *Model Evaluation (Cross-Validation, ROC Curves, Precision-Recall)*
  - **Day 41-50:** *Data Engineering (Feature Engineering, Big Data Tools)*
  - **Day 51-60:** *Deep Learning (CNNs, RNNs, Transformers)*
  - **Day 61-70:** *Practical Applications (NLP, Computer Vision, AI Ethics)*
  - **Day 71-75:** *Interview Preparation and Mock Interviews*

Part IV: The Resolution

CHAPTER: THE RESOLUTION

- **CHECRET WOBEITS:** few Prptöersonte ah faradah Lnink ollish kit fabotaejaue's for aronesl & evinetoge ery eerd sondlaö.

- **PREPARONG** kegha us oil bolleren, thei suecivier this adtientilee and utadels aiase arew ite krour outh for echers use tder caide.

- **CHECKEK ONIONS:** This boevel whic'/e wellow 'saint be-w athea likle sha lean aee enelvissfuls seliiasessniry and he As rast elegisterd enter cinihe n, enal Wer silleg Dread.

- **OUTDEI 11** On phe. ICedeful durgoral until w fith lleat fottid.:s leval doestionstip ane-to bai tth reall turges for the ble ture.

- **COCFISITN:** Wed joth The Ivey-fofogr oh taroaw the stoat her, wfillarne

- Atyii prukre a nshe, be aljoee or 'kringeo sour shlli o-ee be and sil famed, a bookql'tinii rea it out or g q·ar, bulle hepp'ggliver.

- **EXPCRVES fIRANBNG, FRIS Disif 610D** of othn nore goofinitee'ivq baringe And nilangt and the idogti spandu togehed.

- oss un on ar tavke foor oleetivery, oh jot its (he. witchliing 'uspeat (Θerñeir end)) ther tood, but loge tath

- **STEAPISER g:vb a** on am pient Zaothy sew, hulamser sTil the cha'e: huck,, the t's congeneal, drssevee.

Chapter 9: The Interview

- Both Aditi and Arjun prepare for their interviews using the knowledge gained.
- Detailed preparation and successful interviews are depicted.

Chapter 10: The Union

- Their successful professional achievements lead to a stronger personal bond.
- They reconcile their past misunderstandings and look forward to a future together.

Chapter 11: Khamoshi Revisited

- *Reflect on their journey, the significance of silence in their relationship, and the lessons learned.*
- *Conclude with their commitment to each other, blending love, career, and shared dreams.*
-

Interview Guide

Basics:

1. Statistics & Probability:
    - Explain mean, median, mode, and standard deviation.

- Discuss probability distributions (normal, binomial).

2. **Data Cleaning:**
   - Describe techniques for handling missing data.
   - Discuss outlier detection and treatment.

3. **Introduction to Machine Learning:**
   - Define supervised and unsupervised learning.
   - Explain overfitting vs. underfitting.

Intermediate:

4. **Algorithms:**
   - Explain decision trees and how they work.
   - Discuss the concept of k-nearest neighbors (k-NN).

5. **Model Evaluation:**
   - Describe cross-validation techniques.
   - Explain precision, recall, and F1-score.

6. **Feature Engineering:**
   - Discuss feature scaling and normalization.
   - Explain dimensionality reduction techniques (PCA).

Advanced:

7. **Deep Learning:**
   - Describe the architecture of neural networks.
   - Explain convolutional neural networks (CNNs) and their applications.

8. Natural Language Processing (NLP):
- Discuss text processing and sentiment analysis.
- Explain the concept of transformers and attention mechanisms.

9. AI Ethics:
- Discuss ethical considerations in AI and data privacy.
- Explain bias and fairness in machine learning models.

Interview Prep:

10. Mock Interviews:
- Conduct practice interviews with common data science questions.
- Provide feedback and tips for improvement.

Conclusion:

Khamoshi: Echoes of Silence is a narrative that blends professional growth with personal connection, demonstrating how love and learning can intertwine to create a meaningful and enduring relationship. Aditi and Arjun's story serves as a testament to the power of shared passions and the importance of communication in overcoming challenges.

Chapter 1: The Meeting

Aditi Sharma adjusted her glasses and scanned the bustling conference hall. The room was abuzz with the energy of over a thousand data science enthusiasts gathered for the annual AI Innovators Conference. The event was known for its keynote speakers, groundbreaking research presentations, and myriad networking opportunities. Aditi was no stranger to such events; her passion for data science had led her to conferences all over the world. However, this particular day felt different. It was as if the universe had orchestrated something extraordinary just for her.

Aditi, a rising star in the field of artificial intelligence, had just finished her presentation on the latest advancements in reinforcement learning. The crowd's reception had been overwhelmingly positive, with many attendees eager to discuss her work further. Her presentation had showcased how adaptive learning algorithms could optimize robotic control systems, a topic that merged theory with practical application in an exciting way.

After the presentation, Aditi took a deep breath, relieved and exhilarated. She grabbed a cup of coffee and walked towards the refreshments table. As she sipped her coffee, she overheard snippets of conversation about an upcoming session on advanced neural networks. Her interest piqued, she decided to attend the session.

Meanwhile, Arjun Patel was at the opposite end of the hall, immersed in a discussion with a colleague about the potential of generative adversarial networks (GANs) in creating synthetic data for training AI models. Arjun, known for his innovative work on GANs, had just wrapped up his own talk about the future of AI in creative applications. He was excited about the potential for AI to revolutionize fields like art and music, and his passion was evident as he animatedly explained his latest research.

As the session on neural networks began, Aditi found a seat towards the middle of the room, her mind already brimming with questions. The speaker, a well-respected figure in the AI community, was discussing cutting-edge techniques in deep learning. Aditi's focus was unwavering, and she took detailed notes, her curiosity driving her to absorb every bit of information.

Arjun entered the room just as the session was starting to delve into the technical details of convolutional neural networks (CNNs). He scanned the room, and his gaze settled on Aditi, who was intently taking notes. Something about her focused demeanor intrigued him. He had seen many experts in the field, but there was something different about her approach. Deciding to sit nearby, he hoped to catch a few insights from the session and maybe strike up a conversation later.

The session progressed, and Aditi found herself lost in the complexities of the discussion. Suddenly, a hand tapped her on the shoulder. Startled, she turned to see Arjun smiling at her.

"Hi," he said. "I couldn't help but notice how engaged you are. I'm Arjun."

Aditi smiled back, slightly taken aback but pleased by the interaction. "Hi, Arjun. I'm Aditi. I'm just trying to absorb as much as I can from this session."

Arjun chuckled. "I know the feeling. I've been following your work on reinforcement learning. It's impressive."

Aditi's eyes widened. "Really? That means a lot coming from someone who's done such pioneering work with GANs. I've read your papers too. They're quite inspiring."

The two quickly fell into an animated discussion about their respective fields. The session continued around them, but they barely noticed as they delved into a deep conversation about the future of AI. They exchanged ideas about the integration of different AI techniques and their potential impact on various industries.

Their conversation flowed effortlessly, each exchange revealing a mutual respect and admiration for the other's work. They found themselves discussing not just their research but also their visions for the future of AI. The discussion ranged from theoretical debates to practical applications, each topic leading to another with increasing excitement.

The session ended, and the room began to clear out. Aditi and Arjun, still engrossed in conversation, decided to grab a seat at a nearby café to continue their discussion. As they walked towards the café, they both felt a palpable sense of connection. It wasn't just the professional respect they held for each other but also an undercurrent of personal resonance.

At the café, they ordered coffee and settled into a corner table. Arjun, ever the conversationalist, initiated a discussion about the challenges and opportunities in AI research. Aditi responded with her own insights, revealing her passion for the field and her dreams of creating AI systems that could significantly impact real-world problems.

As the conversation deepened, Aditi shared her recent project on adaptive learning algorithms for autonomous vehicles. Arjun, equally passionate, talked about his latest work on improving the efficiency of GANs for generating high-quality synthetic data. They realized they had a lot in common—not just in their research interests but also in their approach to problem-solving and innovation.

Their conversation took a turn when Arjun mentioned a recent breakthrough in his work that he was particularly excited about. Aditi listened intently, her eyes lighting up with genuine interest. "That's fascinating," she said. "I've been exploring similar techniques for my own project. Maybe there's an opportunity for us to collaborate."

Arjun's eyes sparkled with enthusiasm. "I'd love that. It's always exciting to work with someone who shares a similar vision."

The idea of collaboration opened up a new avenue for both of them. They exchanged contact details, promising to continue their discussion and explore potential research opportunities together. As they parted ways, both felt a sense of anticipation and excitement about what the future might hold.

As Aditi walked back to her hotel, she reflected on the day's events. Meeting Arjun had been an unexpected delight. His knowledge, passion, and enthusiasm for AI mirrored her own, and the prospect of working together on innovative projects was exhilarating. She had always believed that true collaboration could lead to groundbreaking advancements, and she felt that her encounter with Arjun could be the beginning of something special.

Arjun, on the other hand, was equally thrilled. His conversation with Aditi had been a breath of fresh air. Her insights and ideas were not only thought-provoking but also aligned with his own aspirations in the field. He admired her dedication and was eager to see where their discussions and potential collaboration could lead.

As the days passed, Aditi and Arjun continued their discussions through emails and video calls. Their professional connection deepened, and they found themselves growing more interested in each other's work and ideas. Their conversations were filled with a blend of technical discussions and personal reflections, creating a bond that went beyond mere professional courtesy.

The initial meeting at the conference had set the stage for a promising partnership. Little did they know that their journey together would be marked by both personal and professional twists and turns, leading them into a world of shared dreams, challenges, and unexpected revelations.

As they prepared for their next collaborative project, both Aditi and Arjun felt a sense of anticipation and excitement. Their paths had crossed in a way that felt both serendipitous and destined. The future was filled with possibilities, and they were ready to explore them together, driven by their passion for AI and their growing connection.

Chapter 2: Data Science and Love

Aditi and Arjun's initial conversation at the AI Innovators Conference had set a foundation for what both of them hoped would be a fruitful collaboration. In the weeks following the conference, their discussions moved from theoretical debates and research ideas to practical applications and potential projects. Their mutual admiration for each other's work soon blossomed into a tangible partnership.

1. The Genesis of Collaboration

The first official step towards their collaboration came in the form of a project proposal. Aditi had been working on a research project focusing on enhancing reinforcement learning algorithms for autonomous systems, aiming to make them more adaptive and efficient. Arjun, on the other hand, was exploring novel ways to apply Generative Adversarial Networks (GANs) to create realistic simulations for training AI models.

During one of their regular video calls, Aditi broached the idea of integrating their research. "Arjun," she began, her tone filled with excitement, "I've been thinking about how your work with GANs could complement my project on reinforcement learning. Imagine using GAN-generated data to simulate more complex environments for autonomous systems. It could drastically improve the training efficiency."

Arjun's eyes lit up. "That's a brilliant idea, Aditi! The realism that GANs can bring to simulations would definitely push the boundaries of reinforcement learning. Let's draft a proposal and see if we can get it funded."

They spent the next few weeks drafting a detailed research proposal. Their emails and messages were filled with technical discussions, data models, and theoretical insights. What started as a professional exchange soon became a series of collaborative efforts that were both intellectually stimulating and deeply engaging.

2. Building the Research Framework

Their project began to take shape as they outlined the objectives, methodologies, and expected outcomes. They decided to use GANs to generate synthetic environments that could challenge and refine their reinforcement learning algorithms. The idea was to create dynamic, unpredictable environments where autonomous systems could learn and adapt more robustly.

One late evening, as they worked on refining their project proposal, Aditi found herself reflecting on their growing professional relationship. The discussions with Arjun were always insightful and filled with a kind of intellectual chemistry she hadn't experienced before. His approach to problem-solving and his enthusiasm for exploring new ideas resonated deeply with her.

"Arjun," she typed, her fingers hovering over the keyboard, "I have to say, working with you on this project has been incredibly rewarding. Your perspective on using GANs for simulation has opened up new possibilities for my research."

Arjun's response came quickly. "I feel the same way, Aditi. Your innovative ideas and deep understanding of reinforcement learning have really pushed me to think outside the box. It's rare to find a collaborator who matches your passion and drive."

Their correspondence soon included more personal exchanges. They shared stories about their experiences in the field, their aspirations, and even their challenges. Each interaction strengthened their bond, both professionally and personally.

3. The First Meeting Post-Proposal

With the proposal accepted and funded, Aditi and Arjun planned their first face-to-face meeting to kick off their collaboration. They chose a quiet café in downtown San Francisco, a place with a cozy atmosphere that seemed perfect for both work and conversation.

As Aditi walked into the café, she spotted Arjun already seated at a corner table, engrossed in his laptop. He looked up as she approached, and a warm smile spread across his face. "Aditi! It's great to finally meet in person."

Aditi returned the smile, feeling a flutter of excitement. "Arjun, it's good to see you too."

They exchanged pleasantries and began discussing the project in more detail. As they delved into the technical aspects of their research, their conversation flowed seamlessly. They reviewed their project plan, fine-tuned their objectives, and brainstormed potential challenges and solutions.

Over coffee and pastries, their discussion took on a more personal tone. They talked about their backgrounds, their journeys into the field of AI, and their passions beyond research. It was during these moments that they discovered a shared love for classical music, hiking, and a penchant for late-night brainstorming sessions.

Aditi found herself increasingly drawn to Arjun's charisma and intellect. His thoughtful approach and genuine curiosity made every conversation engaging. Similarly, Arjun admired Aditi's dedication and creativity. Her ability to articulate complex ideas with clarity and passion was both inspiring and captivating.

4. The Depth of Connection

As the project progressed, their interactions became more frequent. They collaborated closely, exchanging ideas, analyzing data, and refining their models. Their professional relationship continued to grow, and so did their personal connection.

One evening, after a particularly productive day of coding and model testing, Arjun suggested they take a break. "How about we go for a walk? There's a beautiful park nearby."

Aditi, feeling both exhilarated and curious, agreed. As they walked through the park, the conversation naturally shifted from technical topics to more personal matters. They talked about their dreams, their fears, and their perspectives on life.

Arjun, with a hint of hesitation, shared his experiences of overcoming challenges in his career. "There were times when I felt like giving up, but the support from colleagues and the excitement of discovery kept me going."

Aditi listened intently, her admiration for Arjun deepening. "I've faced similar challenges. It's moments like these that remind us why we're passionate about what we do."

Their conversation was punctuated by laughter and moments of reflective silence. The ease with which they communicated and the depth of their connection were undeniable. By the time they returned from the walk, both felt a stronger bond than before.

5. Moments of Intimacy

As the weeks went by, their professional and personal interactions continued to intertwine. They shared more moments of intimacy, both intellectual and emotional. They celebrated each other's achievements, supported each other through setbacks, and enjoyed each other's company.

One evening, while working late in Aditi's lab, Arjun glanced at her with a hint of playfulness. "You know, Aditi, I've always wondered if there's a way to measure the 'chemistry' between collaborators. I'd bet our score would be off the charts."

Aditi laughed, her eyes sparkling. "I'd agree. It's rare to find someone who not only understands the intricacies of data science but also shares a similar sense of humor."

Their playful banter and shared moments of joy were becoming an integral part of their relationship. They found themselves increasingly drawn to each other, not just as collaborators but as friends who enjoyed each other's company.

6. The Realization

One night, after a particularly intense coding session, Aditi and Arjun sat together in a quiet corner of a café, their laptops closed and their coffee cups empty. The air was filled with a sense of accomplishment and contentment.

Arjun looked at Aditi, his expression serious yet tender. "Aditi, I've been meaning to tell you something. Working with you has been more than just a professional experience for me. I've come to value our time together, both the discussions and the moments we share outside of work."

Aditi's heart skipped a beat. She had been feeling the same way but had hesitated to express it. "I feel the same, Arjun. Our collaboration has been incredibly rewarding, and our personal connection means a lot to me."

Their mutual feelings were finally out in the open, and the realization brought a sense of relief and joy. They both knew that their relationship had grown beyond the confines of a professional partnership. The connection they shared was deep and genuine, and they were both excited about the possibilities of exploring it further.

7. A New Chapter

As their project advanced, so did their relationship. They continued to work closely, pushing the boundaries of their research while nurturing their growing bond. Their shared passion for data science and their personal connection created a unique synergy, driving them both to new heights.

Their collaboration became a testament to the power of combining professional expertise with personal connection. The success of their project was not only a reflection of their hard work but also a celebration of their journey together.

As they wrapped up their project and prepared for the next phase of their work, Aditi and Arjun looked forward to the future with a sense of excitement and anticipation. Their partnership had evolved into something meaningful and enduring, and they were eager to continue their journey together, both as collaborators and as partners in a deeper, more personal sense.

The collaboration between Aditi and Arjun was more than just a professional endeavor; it was the beginning of a profound and evolving relationship. Their shared passion for data science had brought them together, and their intellectual and emotional connection had set the stage for a journey filled with discovery, growth, and love.

Chapter 3: The Spark of Romance

The months following the successful launch of their joint research project were a whirlwind of activity and accomplishment for Aditi and Arjun. Their professional relationship had flourished, marked by late-night coding sessions, breakthrough moments, and collaborative triumphs. As they navigated the

complexities of their research, a new dimension began to weave itself into their connection—one that transcended the boundaries of their professional partnership.

1. Late-Night Revelations

One crisp autumn evening, Aditi and Arjun were working late in Aditi's lab, their eyes focused on the screens that displayed lines of code and complex data visualizations. The room was illuminated by the soft glow of computer monitors, casting long shadows that danced on the walls. The hum of the lab's air conditioning was the only sound, punctuated occasionally by the clacking of keyboards.

Aditi, stretching her arms after a particularly intense coding session, glanced over at Arjun. His face was illuminated by the screen, his concentration evident. "I think we've made significant progress tonight," she said, her voice breaking the silence.

Arjun looked up, his eyes meeting hers with a tired yet satisfied expression. "Absolutely. It's amazing how our models are starting to show real promise."

There was a brief pause as both reflected on their progress. Aditi took a sip of her coffee and then turned to Arjun with a playful glint in her eye. "Do you remember when we first started this project? I never imagined we'd get this far."

Arjun smiled, his gaze softening. "Neither did I. But I'm glad we did. This project has been one of the most rewarding experiences of my career, not just because of the research, but because of the people I've worked with."

Aditi felt a flutter in her chest. There was something about the way Arjun spoke, the sincerity in his voice, that resonated deeply with her. "I feel the same way, Arjun. It's not just the project—it's the connection we've built along the way."

The air between them seemed to shift, and Aditi felt a growing awareness of the moment's intimacy. She could see the admiration in Arjun's eyes and sensed a mutual acknowledgment of something more than professional camaraderie.

2. Exploring New Dimensions

The following weeks were marked by a series of moments that gradually unveiled the burgeoning romance between Aditi and Arjun. Their professional interactions remained as productive and collaborative as ever, but a subtle shift in their dynamic began to emerge.

One weekend, after completing a major milestone in their project, Arjun suggested they take a break and celebrate. "How about we go out for dinner? We've been working non-stop, and I think we deserve a little celebration."

Aditi agreed with a smile. "That sounds perfect. I've been craving a good meal and some time away from the lab."

They chose a cozy restaurant known for its ambiance and delicious cuisine. As they settled into a corner table, the soft music and candlelight created a warm and intimate atmosphere. The conversation flowed effortlessly as they talked about their favorite foods, travel experiences, and future aspirations.

During the dinner, Arjun couldn't help but notice how naturally the conversation flowed. Aditi's laughter, her thoughtful insights, and her easygoing nature made the evening enjoyable and relaxed. He found himself increasingly captivated by her presence.

At the end of the meal, as they walked out of the restaurant, Arjun took a moment to express his appreciation. "Aditi, I just wanted to say how much I've enjoyed our time together. Not just tonight, but throughout this project. It's been truly special."

Aditi's heart skipped a beat. She had been feeling the same way but had hesitated to voice it. "I've enjoyed it too, Arjun. More than I expected."

Their eyes met in the dim light of the street, and there was a moment of silent understanding. The connection they shared was palpable, and the evening had deepened their feelings for each other.

3. Moments of Intimacy

As their project continued, Aditi and Arjun found themselves spending more time together outside of work. They began to share personal experiences, hobbies, and even quiet moments of reflection.

One afternoon, while working in Aditi's lab, they decided to take a break and enjoy the city's autumn beauty. They strolled through a nearby park, the fallen leaves crunching beneath their feet.

Arjun, with a playful grin, picked up a handful of leaves and tossed them gently towards Aditi. "Do you remember doing this as a kid?"

Aditi laughed, catching a leaf in mid-air. "Absolutely. It's been a while since I did something this carefree."

Their walk through the park was filled with light-hearted conversation and shared laughter. They discussed their favorite childhood memories, their dreams for the future, and their personal passions. Each topic revealed more about their personalities and brought them closer together.

As they sat on a bench, watching the sunset, Arjun turned to Aditi with a thoughtful expression. "You know, I've realized that our conversations have become some of the highlights of my day. It's not just about the research; it's about getting to know you."

Aditi felt a warm glow inside her. "I feel the same way. There's something really special about our connection."

The tenderness in their conversation was undeniable, and they both felt a growing sense of intimacy. The spark of romance was becoming more apparent, and they were both keenly aware of the deepening bond between them.

4. The Confession

As their feelings for each other grew stronger, there were moments of vulnerability and confession. One evening, after a particularly challenging day at work, Arjun and Aditi found themselves alone in her apartment, reviewing some data on her laptop.

Arjun, his face reflecting a mix of fatigue and contemplation, looked at Aditi. "I've been meaning to talk to you about something. It's been on my mind for a while."

Aditi looked up from the laptop, her curiosity piqued. "What's on your mind?"

Arjun took a deep breath, his eyes meeting hers. "I've been thinking about how much our relationship has evolved. Working with you has been one of the most rewarding experiences of my career. But beyond that, I've realized that my feelings for you have grown into something deeper."

Aditi's heart raced. She had been grappling with similar feelings but had been unsure how to express them. "Arjun, I've been feeling the same way. Our time together has meant so much to me, both professionally and personally."

The admission was met with a moment of silence, as both processed the significance of their words. Arjun reached out and gently took Aditi's hand. "I care about you a lot, Aditi. More than I ever expected."

Aditi's eyes softened as she squeezed his hand. "I care about you too, Arjun. Our connection is something I value deeply."

Their shared confession marked a turning point in their relationship. The feelings they had both harbored in the quiet moments and the late-night discussions were now openly acknowledged. The spark of romance that had been growing was now a flame, and they were both eager to explore where it might lead.

5. Embracing the Future

With their feelings for each other openly acknowledged, Aditi and Arjun began to explore their relationship in a new light. They continued to work closely on their research project, but their interactions were now infused with a sense of shared affection and deeper connection.

Their time together was filled with moments of tenderness, whether it was a shared smile during a coding breakthrough or a quiet conversation over dinner. They supported each other through the highs and lows of their work, and their bond grew stronger with each passing day.

One evening, after a particularly successful presentation of their research findings, Arjun and Aditi celebrated with a quiet dinner at a favorite restaurant. As they clinked glasses in a toast, Arjun looked at Aditi with a sense of contentment. "Here's to us—our work, our connection, and the future we're building together."

Aditi smiled, her heart full. "To us."

Their relationship had become a blend of professional collaboration and personal romance, creating a unique and fulfilling partnership. They looked forward to the future with a sense of excitement and anticipation, knowing that their journey together was just beginning.

6. Navigating the Balance

As they navigated their evolving relationship, Aditi and Arjun faced the challenge of balancing their professional and personal lives. They were determined to maintain the integrity of their work while nurturing their romantic connection.

One afternoon, as they worked in Arjun's office, Aditi brought up the topic. "Arjun, I've been thinking about how we can maintain a balance between our work and personal lives. It's important to me that we continue to support each other professionally while also nurturing our relationship."

Arjun nodded in agreement. "I've been thinking about that too. It's crucial that we keep our professional interactions focused and productive while also making time for our personal connection."

They discussed strategies for managing their time and maintaining clear boundaries between work and personal life. Their commitment to each other and their project was unwavering, and they were determined to make their relationship work in both spheres.

7. A New Beginning

As they embarked on new phases of their research and personal lives, Aditi and Arjun were filled with a sense of optimism and excitement. Their journey together had been marked by professional achievements and personal growth, and they were eager to see where their relationship would take them.

Their shared passion for data science and their deepening bond had created a unique and fulfilling partnership. They looked forward to exploring new opportunities, both in their research and in their lives together.

As they continued to work side by side, their connection only grew stronger. Their love story was intertwined with their professional success, creating a beautiful and harmonious blend of passion, intellect, and affection.

With each new day, Aditi and Arjun embraced the challenges and joys of their journey, confident that their partnership was built on a foundation of mutual respect, shared dreams, and a deep, enduring love.

The spark of romance between Aditi and Arjun had ignited a new chapter in their lives. Their relationship was a testament to the power of combining professional collaboration with personal connection. As they continued to work together and explore their feelings, they looked forward to a future filled with promise and possibility. Their journey had only just begun, and they were excited to see where their love and their shared passion for data science would lead them.

Chapter 4: Misunderstandings

The leaves had turned golden and crisp, and the days were growing shorter as autumn deepened into winter. The world outside seemed to be preparing for a season of reflection and rest, but inside Aditi and Arjun's lab, the pace was anything but slow. Their joint project, which had started with such promise and enthusiasm, had reached a critical juncture. Deadlines loomed, and the pressure was mounting.

1. The Unspoken Tensions

It was a chilly November morning when the first signs of trouble began to surface. Aditi arrived at the lab earlier than usual, hoping to get a head start on some data analysis. She had been feeling increasingly stressed about the project deadlines, and her sleep had been disrupted by nagging thoughts of pending tasks and looming deliverables.

Arjun, on the other hand, had been working late the previous night. He had stayed up coding and debugging, convinced that his late-night efforts would bring the breakthrough they needed. When he finally arrived at the lab, he was exhausted but determined.

"Good morning, Arjun," Aditi said, trying to keep her tone upbeat. "How did the coding go last night?"

Arjun, bleary-eyed but resolute, replied, "It's been a rough night. I think I've made some progress, but I'm not quite sure yet. I'm hoping we can go over it together."

Aditi nodded, her anxiety barely hidden behind her professional demeanor. "Sure, let's review the results and see where we stand."

As they delved into their work, Aditi couldn't shake the feeling that something was off. The data wasn't aligning as they had hoped, and Arjun's fatigue seemed to affect his focus. Their conversations, once fluid and filled with intellectual excitement, had become terse and fragmented.

The tension between them was palpable, though neither acknowledged it openly. They worked through the morning and into the afternoon, but the stress of their looming deadlines and the misalignment in their work began to strain their interactions.

2. The Catalyst for Conflict

It wasn't until the following week that the issue came to a head. They were preparing for a crucial presentation to a potential investor, and the pressure to deliver results was intense. Both Aditi and Arjun had been working non-stop, their schedules packed with meetings, coding sessions, and endless revisions.

One afternoon, Aditi received an email from their project coordinator. The email included revised deadlines for their deliverables, which were significantly earlier than they had originally anticipated. The new timeline was a shock, and Aditi felt her heart sink as she read through the details.

Feeling a surge of anxiety, Aditi decided to bring it up with Arjun immediately. "Arjun, we need to talk," she said, her voice trembling slightly as she approached him in his office.

Arjun, lost in his own world of code and graphs, looked up with a mixture of curiosity and fatigue. "What's up?"

Aditi showed him the email, her expression tight. "The deadlines have been moved up. We have to deliver our results much sooner than expected. This is going to put a lot of pressure on us."

Arjun's face fell as he read through the email. "This is unexpected. We've barely had time to get the data we need. How are we supposed to meet these new deadlines?"

Aditi's frustration was evident. "I don't know, but we need to come up with a plan. We can't afford to miss this opportunity."

Arjun, feeling overwhelmed, ran a hand through his hair. "I've been working non-stop, and I'm already behind on my part. I don't see how we're going to make it."

The conversation quickly escalated into an argument. Aditi's anxiety and Arjun's exhaustion collided, creating a storm of emotions. "Maybe if we had been more organized from the start, we wouldn't be in this mess," Aditi said, her frustration boiling over.

Arjun's response was sharp. "It's easy to blame each other, but we're both under pressure. I'm doing my best, but I can't do everything."

The argument left both of them feeling hurt and misunderstood. They ended the discussion with a sense of unresolved tension and frustration, retreating into their individual corners of the lab.

3. The Silence That Followed

In the days that followed, the once-close bond between Aditi and Arjun seemed to fracture. They continued to work together, but their interactions were marked by a cold professionalism. The warmth and camaraderie they had once shared were replaced by a silent distance.

Aditi spent her days buried in data analysis, her thoughts consumed by the project's mounting challenges. She avoided making eye contact with Arjun, focusing solely on her work. The silence between them was heavy, and the emotional distance was palpable.

Arjun, too, was consumed by his tasks. He worked long hours, hoping that the extra effort would somehow alleviate the pressure. But the strain of their argument lingered, and he found himself struggling to maintain his usual focus and enthusiasm.

One evening, as Aditi worked late into the night, she received a message from Arjun. It was brief and business-like, asking for an update on her progress. The message was a stark reminder of their strained relationship, and Aditi felt a pang of sadness as she replied with the requested information.

The silence continued for days, each of them lost in their own world of stress and frustration. The emotional distance between them grew, and their once-easy conversations became rare and strained.

4. The Turning Point

The turning point came unexpectedly. Aditi had been working on a particularly difficult piece of data when she received a phone call from a friend. Her friend's cheerful voice and supportive words provided a much-needed respite from the tension she had been feeling.

During the call, Aditi realized how much she missed the connection she had shared with Arjun. The warmth and understanding that had once characterized their relationship seemed like a distant memory. She felt a surge of regret for the way things had turned out.

Determined to address the situation, Aditi decided to reach out to Arjun. She knew that they needed to have an honest conversation if they were to overcome their misunderstandings.

She found Arjun in his office, surrounded by papers and empty coffee cups. The exhaustion on his face mirrored her own. "Arjun, can we talk?" she asked, her voice steady but gentle.

Arjun looked up, his eyes reflecting a mixture of surprise and weariness. "Sure, Aditi. What's on your mind?"

5. The Heart-to-Heart Conversation

They met in the small break room of the lab, away from the clutter of their workspaces. The room was quiet, and the soft hum of the refrigerator provided a soothing backdrop to their conversation.

Aditi took a deep breath and began. "Arjun, I've been thinking about our argument and the way things have been between us. I realize now that I let my stress and frustration get the better of me. I'm sorry for how I reacted."

Arjun's expression softened. "I'm sorry too, Aditi. I've been feeling overwhelmed and frustrated, and I didn't handle it well either. I should have communicated better instead of letting things fester."

The conversation was a turning point. They both acknowledged their feelings and took responsibility for their part in the conflict. They discussed the challenges they had been facing and how they could better support each other moving forward.

"I think we need to find a way to manage our stress and communicate more openly," Aditi said. "We're in this together, and we need to support each other."

Arjun nodded in agreement. "Absolutely. We've always been a strong team, and I believe we can get through this if we work together and keep talking."

The conversation was a cathartic release for both of them. They shared their frustrations, their fears, and their hopes for the future. By the end of their discussion, the tension that had once clouded their relationship had begun to lift.

6. Rebuilding the Connection

With their hearts laid bare, Aditi and Arjun began the process of rebuilding their connection. They made a conscious effort to communicate more openly and support each other through the challenges they faced.

They implemented new strategies to manage their workload and reduce stress. They scheduled regular check-ins to discuss their progress and address any concerns before they escalated into conflicts. They also made time for short breaks and moments of relaxation, recognizing the importance of balancing work and personal well-being.

As they worked through their project, they rediscovered the joy of collaborating and the warmth of their connection. Their interactions became more relaxed and genuine, and the emotional distance that had crept in began to close.

One evening, after a productive day of work, Aditi and Arjun decided to take a break and enjoy a quiet dinner together. They chose a cozy restaurant with a relaxed atmosphere, where they could unwind and reconnect.

Over dinner, they shared stories and laughter, reminiscing about their earlier days of collaboration. The conversation flowed effortlessly, and they both felt a renewed sense of closeness.

"I'm really glad we had that talk," Aditi said, her eyes reflecting a sense of contentment. "It's made a huge difference in how we work together."

Arjun smiled, his eyes meeting hers with warmth. "Me too. It's reminded me of why we make such a great team. We've got a lot to offer each other, both professionally and personally."

As they clinked glasses in a toast, they felt a sense of optimism and renewed commitment. The challenges they had faced had only strengthened their bond and deepened their understanding of each other.

7. Moving Forward

With their renewed connection and improved communication, Aditi and Arjun continued to navigate the complexities of their project and their relationship. They embraced the lessons learned from their misunderstandings and applied them to both their work and their personal lives.

Their journey was not without its challenges, but they approached each obstacle with a sense of partnership and resilience. The experience had taught them the importance of openness, empathy, and mutual support.

As they worked together on their project, their relationship flourished. They continued to share their passions, support each other's goals, and celebrate their successes. Their bond, forged through both triumphs and trials, became a source of strength and inspiration.

The season of autumn slowly gave way to winter, and with it came a sense of renewal and hope. Aditi and Arjun faced the future with confidence, knowing that their relationship was built on a foundation of understanding, respect, and love.

Their journey was far from over, but they were ready to embrace the next chapter with a sense of excitement and possibility. Together, they had weathered the storm of misunderstanding and emerged stronger, more connected, and more determined than ever to achieve their shared dreams.

In this chapter, the emotional and professional challenges faced by Aditi and Arjun serve as a poignant reminder of the complexities of both relationships and collaborative work. Their journey through misunderstandings and their efforts to rebuild their connection highlight the importance of communication, empathy, and mutual support in overcoming obstacles and nurturing a lasting bond.

Chapter 5: The Silence

The late autumn days were marked by an air of frosty silence, both outside and within Aditi and Arjun's lives. The colorful hues of the leaves had given way to bare branches, and the chill in the air seemed to reflect the coldness that had settled between them. After their argument over the project deadlines, the once warm and collaborative environment in the lab had turned into a sterile and tense space.

1. The Decision to Withdraw

The argument that had transpired had left both Aditi and Arjun feeling raw and exposed. The harsh words spoken and the emotional distance that followed had created a chasm that neither knew how to bridge. In the immediate aftermath, both had retreated into themselves, their pride and hurt preventing them from reaching out to one another.

Aditi, feeling a mix of anger and sadness, made the decision to withdraw from communication. She focused on her work with a renewed intensity, hoping that immersing herself in data analysis would help her forget the emotional turmoil. She threw herself into her tasks, hoping that the work would provide a distraction from the personal pain.

Arjun, similarly affected by the argument, chose to isolate himself. He buried himself in code and technical problems, using the complexity of his work as a shield against his feelings. He avoided eye contact with Aditi, and their interactions in the lab became curt and professional. The silence between them was both a defense mechanism and a source of distress.

2. Internal Struggles

As the days of silence stretched into weeks, both Aditi and Arjun grappled with their internal struggles. The lack of communication left them with ample time to reflect on their actions and emotions, and the process of self-examination was both painful and revealing.

Aditi's Internal Struggles

Aditi found herself plagued by doubts and regrets. The silence that had followed the argument was deafening, and she could not escape the nagging feeling that something essential had been lost. Her mind replayed the argument in a loop, questioning her responses and the choices she had made.

One evening, after a particularly grueling day at work, Aditi sat alone in her apartment, staring out of the window at the darkening sky. The city lights below flickered, but they offered no comfort. Her thoughts turned inward, and she began to question the future of her relationship with Arjun.

She reflected on their journey together—the excitement of their initial meetings, the late-night brainstorming sessions, and the moments of shared laughter. It was clear to her that the emotional connection they had once shared was precious, and she felt a deep sense of loss at how things had unraveled.

Aditi's inner dialogue was filled with self-reproach. She wondered if she had been too quick to anger, if she had failed to see Arjun's perspective, or if she had been too rigid in her expectations. The silence, though initially a relief from the emotional turmoil, had become a source of introspection and self-criticism.

She spent hours jotting down her thoughts in a journal, attempting to make sense of her feelings. The pages were filled with emotional outpourings, questions without answers, and a longing for resolution. Despite her best efforts to focus on her work, her mind often wandered back to Arjun, and she felt a deep ache for the connection they had once shared.

Arjun's Internal Struggles

Arjun's internal struggles mirrored Aditi's in many ways. The silence that had followed their argument was a heavy burden, and he found himself wrestling with feelings of frustration, guilt, and confusion. His work, which had once been a source of fulfillment, now felt like an endless treadmill of tasks and deadlines.

He spent long hours in his office, his face illuminated by the glow of his computer screen. Despite his efforts to focus on coding and problem-solving, he was haunted by thoughts of Aditi and their fractured relationship. The silence had created an emotional void, and Arjun felt lost and disoriented.

In his quieter moments, Arjun reflected on the nature of their argument. He wondered if he had been too stubborn, too defensive, or too absorbed in his own stress to truly understand Aditi's perspective. He regretted the way their communication had deteriorated and felt a deep sense of guilt for not reaching out to mend things.

Arjun's thoughts often turned to the future of their project and their personal relationship. He questioned whether they could overcome the barriers that had been erected between them. The silence had created a chasm that seemed insurmountable, and he struggled with feelings of helplessness and despair.

3. The Impact on Their Work

The period of silence had a noticeable impact on their work. The project, which had once been a source of excitement and achievement, now felt like a burden. The lack of communication between Aditi and Arjun meant that important decisions were left unmade, and their progress began to slow.

Aditi's work was marked by a sense of frustration and isolation. She found it difficult to maintain her usual level of productivity, and her once-clear goals became muddled by the emotional weight she was carrying. The data analysis that had once been a source of pleasure now felt like an endless cycle of monotony.

Arjun's coding sessions were similarly affected. The absence of collaboration and support made the work seem more arduous, and he struggled to maintain his focus. The synergy that had characterized their partnership was missing, and the technical problems that had once been manageable now felt overwhelming.

Despite their individual efforts, the project's progress stalled. The deadlines that had once seemed achievable now loomed as insurmountable obstacles. The strain of the situation was evident in their interactions with colleagues and collaborators, who sensed the tension and frustration.

4. Personal Reflections and Growth

As the days of silence continued, both Aditi and Arjun began to experience moments of personal growth and reflection. The isolation forced them to confront their own vulnerabilities and consider the deeper aspects of their relationship.

Aditi's Personal Growth

Aditi's time alone allowed her to gain a deeper understanding of her own emotions and priorities. She began to recognize the importance of communication and empathy in maintaining a healthy relationship. Her reflections led her to acknowledge her own shortcomings and the need for compromise.

In her journal, Aditi wrote about her realization that effective communication was crucial not only for resolving conflicts but also for fostering a strong and supportive partnership. She recognized that her own stress and frustration had contributed to the breakdown in communication and resolved to approach future challenges with a more open and understanding mindset.

Aditi also reflected on the value of the emotional connection she had with Arjun. She understood that their relationship was not just about achieving professional success but also about supporting and nurturing each other through difficult times. The silence had made her appreciate the depth of their bond and the need to work together to overcome obstacles.

Arjun's Personal Growth

For Arjun, the period of silence provided an opportunity for self-examination and growth. He confronted his own fears and insecurities, recognizing the ways in which his own behavior had contributed to the conflict. He reflected on the importance of vulnerability and openness in building a strong and resilient relationship.

Arjun's reflections led him to understand that his tendency to withdraw and isolate himself during times of stress had hindered his ability to connect with others. He realized that true partnership required a willingness to communicate, even when it was difficult. His time alone made him appreciate the need for mutual support and understanding.

In his moments of solitude, Arjun wrote about his hopes for the future and his desire to rebuild the connection with Aditi. He acknowledged the value of their relationship and the importance of working through their differences. His reflections provided him with a renewed sense of purpose and determination to address the issues between them.

5. The Road to Reconciliation

As the two-week period of silence drew to a close, both Aditi and Arjun began to sense a shift in their emotional landscape. The introspection and personal growth they had experienced provided them with new perspectives and a renewed understanding of each other.

One evening, as Aditi sat alone in her apartment, she received a message from Arjun. The message was simple but heartfelt, expressing a desire to meet and talk. The message stirred a mix of hope and apprehension within her.

Aditi decided to respond positively, agreeing to meet with Arjun. She knew that addressing the silence and their unresolved issues was crucial for moving forward.

The prospect of having an open and honest conversation filled her with a sense of cautious optimism.

They arranged to meet at a quiet café they had frequented early in their collaboration. The setting was intimate and relaxed, providing a neutral space for their conversation.

6. The Conversation

When Aditi arrived at the café, she found Arjun waiting at a corner table. His face was a mixture of relief and nervousness, and he stood to greet her with a tentative smile.

"Hi, Aditi," he said softly. "Thanks for meeting me."

Aditi returned the smile, feeling a sense of warmth and vulnerability. "Hi, Arjun. I'm glad we could meet."

They sat down, and the conversation began with a sense of careful exploration. Arjun took a deep breath and started. "I've been doing a lot of thinking over the past couple of weeks. I realize now that our argument and the subsequent silence have been really hard on both of us. I'm sorry for my part in it."

Aditi nodded, her eyes reflecting understanding. "I'm sorry too, Arjun. I've been reflecting on our communication and how we handled the stress. I realize that I let my frustration get the better of me, and I should have been more open with you."

The conversation continued with an open exchange of feelings, regrets, and hopes for the future. They discussed their internal struggles, their realizations, and their commitment to improving their communication and support for each other.

By the end of their conversation, there was a renewed sense of connection and understanding. They acknowledged the challenges they had faced and expressed their determination to move forward together. The silence that had once been a source of pain had become a catalyst for growth and reconciliation.

7. Moving Forward

With their conversation complete, Aditi and Arjun felt a sense of relief and renewed commitment. They agreed to work on their communication and approach future challenges with a greater sense of empathy and collaboration.

As they left the café, they walked side by side, feeling a renewed sense of hope and connection. The road ahead was still uncertain, but they were ready to face it together, armed with a deeper understanding of each other and a shared commitment to their relationship.

The period of silence had been a difficult and painful experience, but it had also provided them with valuable insights and a stronger foundation for their future together. They were determined to embrace the lessons learned and move forward with a renewed sense of partnership and love.

In this chapter, the two-week period of silence serves as a profound exploration of internal struggles and personal growth for both Aditi and Arjun. Their reflections and the eventual reconciliation highlight the importance of communication, empathy, and mutual support in navigating the complexities of relationships and collaborative work. The chapter underscores the *transformative power of confronting and addressing emotional challenges, leading to a stronger and more resilient connection.*

Chapter 6: Breaking the Silence

The snow had begun to fall in gentle flakes, blanketing the city in a soft, white layer. Winter's chill was pervasive, but the warmth of the season's festivities and the promise of renewal hung in the air. The café where

Aditi and Arjun had planned to meet was festively decorated, with twinkling lights and seasonal decorations creating a cozy atmosphere. The space seemed to offer a perfect setting for the conversations that lay ahead.

1. The Reconnection

Aditi arrived at the café early, feeling a blend of anticipation and nervousness. The past two weeks of silence had been an emotional rollercoaster, and she was eager to mend the rift that had formed between her and Arjun. As she settled into a corner table, she took a moment to collect her thoughts, looking out at the falling snow and trying to calm her racing heart.

Arjun arrived shortly after, his face reflecting a mix of apprehension and hope. He spotted Aditi and made his way over, his movements deliberate and thoughtful. When he reached the table, he offered a tentative smile.

"Hi, Aditi," he said softly. "Thanks for meeting me."

Aditi returned the smile, her eyes reflecting a hint of relief. "Hi, Arjun. I'm glad we could finally talk."

They both took their seats, the warmth of the café providing a comforting contrast to the cold outside. The initial moments were marked by a nervous energy, but as they began to speak, the conversation flowed more naturally.

2. Opening Up

Arjun took a deep breath, his fingers tapping lightly on the table. "I've been thinking a lot about our silence and what it means for us. I realized how much I missed our conversations and our connection. It wasn't just the project that was affected; it was us."

Aditi nodded, her gaze steady and empathetic. "I've felt the same way. The silence was hard, and it made me realize how important our relationship is to me. I've been reflecting on what went wrong and how we can fix it."

Arjun leaned forward slightly, his expression earnest. "I want to understand what you've been feeling and how we can move past this. I think it's important for us to talk openly about our emotions and our future."

Aditi took a moment to gather her thoughts before responding. "During our silence, I realized that I've been holding on to a lot of stress and frustration. I let it affect how I communicated with you, and that wasn't fair. I should have been more open about my feelings and less reactive."

Arjun's expression softened as he listened. "I felt the same way. I've been so focused on my own stress that I didn't consider how it was impacting you. I should have reached out sooner and tried to understand your perspective better."

Their conversation delved into the heart of their recent struggles. They spoke candidly about their fears, frustrations, and regrets. Each revelation was met with understanding and empathy, and the conversation became a space of healing and connection.

3. A Deeper Understanding

As their conversation progressed, Aditi and Arjun began to explore deeper aspects of their relationship. They discussed not only their recent issues but also their long-term goals and desires.

Aditi shared her thoughts on the future of their partnership. "I think we need to be more proactive about communicating, especially when we're stressed. We've always been a great team, and I believe we can handle challenges if we work together and support each other."

Arjun nodded in agreement. "I agree. We've accomplished so much together, and I don't want our relationship to suffer because of miscommunication or stress. We need to make an effort to stay connected and be more understanding of each other's needs."

They also talked about their individual goals and how they aligned with their partnership. Arjun expressed his desire to continue advancing their research and making a meaningful impact in the field of AI. Aditi shared her aspirations to contribute to innovative projects and explore new areas of interest.

Through their discussion, they discovered that their personal goals and professional ambitions were complementary. They both valued growth, learning, and collaboration, and their shared vision provided a strong foundation for their future together.

4. Rebuilding Trust and Connection

With their hearts open and their intentions clear, Aditi and Arjun began to discuss ways to rebuild their trust and strengthen their connection. They recognized that trust was essential for a successful partnership, both personally and professionally.

Aditi suggested, "One thing we can do is set aside regular time for check-ins. We can use that time to discuss our progress, address any concerns, and ensure that we're on the same page. It'll help us stay connected and prevent misunderstandings."

Arjun agreed enthusiastically. "That's a great idea. Regular check-ins will give us a chance to address any issues before they become major problems. We can also make time for activities outside of work to maintain our personal connection."

They also agreed to be more open about their feelings and needs. Aditi proposed that they practice active listening, where each would make an effort to understand and validate the other's perspective. Arjun suggested that they establish clear boundaries and expectations to reduce stress and prevent conflicts.

5. Embracing the Future

As their conversation drew to a close, Aditi and Arjun felt a renewed sense of hope and optimism. The period of silence had been challenging, but it had also provided them with valuable insights into their relationship. They were ready to move forward with a deeper understanding of each other and a commitment to nurturing their bond.

Aditi smiled, her eyes reflecting a sense of warmth and determination. "I'm really glad we had this conversation. It's helped me see how important our relationship is and how much I value our connection."

Arjun returned the smile, his expression reflecting a mixture of relief and affection. "Me too. I'm looking forward to moving forward together and making our relationship even stronger."

They left the café, the snowfall outside creating a picturesque scene. As they walked side by side, their conversation continued, filled with laughter and shared dreams. The warmth of their renewed connection seemed to counteract the cold of the winter air.

6. Moving Forward Together

In the weeks that followed, Aditi and Arjun worked diligently to implement the changes they had discussed. Their regular check-ins became a cornerstone of their communication, providing them with a structured way to address any issues and celebrate their successes.

They also made a concerted effort to maintain their personal connection. They scheduled regular outings and activities that allowed them to relax and enjoy each other's company outside of work. These moments of togetherness helped to strengthen their bond and create new, positive memories.

Their project, which had once felt like an overwhelming burden, now became a symbol of their collaborative spirit and commitment to each other. They approached their work with renewed energy and enthusiasm, confident in their ability to overcome challenges as a team.

The period of silence, while difficult, had ultimately brought Aditi and Arjun closer together. It had forced them to confront their vulnerabilities and reaffirm their commitment to each other. The lessons they had learned during this time became an integral part of their relationship, guiding them as they navigated the future.

As winter gradually gave way to spring, Aditi and Arjun looked forward to the new opportunities and adventures that awaited them. Their journey had been marked by challenges and growth, but their love and partnership had emerged stronger than ever.

Their story was a testament to the power of communication, empathy, and resilience. Through their experiences, Aditi and Arjun had discovered the true essence of their relationship and the strength of their connection. They were ready to face the future with confidence, knowing that their love and commitment would guide them through whatever challenges lay ahead.

In this chapter, the process of breaking the silence serves as a pivotal moment for Aditi and Arjun. Their deep and honest conversation allows them to reconnect, address their issues, and reaffirm their commitment to each other. The chapter highlights the importance of communication and empathy in overcoming challenges and strengthening relationships. Through their discussion and renewed efforts, Aditi and Arjun lay the foundation for a future built on mutual understanding and shared goals.

Chapter 7: Data Science Deep Dive

The crisp air of early spring carried a sense of renewal, a fitting backdrop for the new chapter in Aditi and Arjun's relationship. The silence of winter had given way to a dynamic phase of learning and growth, where their personal and professional lives intertwined in the pursuit of knowledge. This chapter was not just about mending their bond but about embarking on a shared journey into the depths of data science. It was a challenge they faced together, combining their passion for AI with their desire to understand each other better.

1. Setting the Stage

The journey began with a clear goal: to enhance their understanding of data science from the ground up. They had both recognized that their knowledge needed a structured framework to address gaps and deepen their expertise. With their previous experience providing a strong foundation, they decided to tackle the subject systematically.

They set up a schedule for their learning journey, dedicating time each day to explore different aspects of data science. The plan was ambitious, covering everything from basic concepts to advanced techniques. Each day had a specific topic, with discussions and exercises designed to reinforce their learning and foster collaboration.

Their days were marked by intense focus and mutual encouragement. They would start their mornings with a brief review of the day's topic, then spend hours diving into research papers, online courses, and practical exercises. Their evenings were reserved for discussions and reflections, where they would share insights, tackle problems, and assess their progress.

2. Day 1-10: Foundations of Data Science

The first few days were dedicated to revisiting the basics of data science. They started with an overview of key concepts and methodologies, including statistics, data wrangling, and exploratory data analysis (EDA).

Day 1: Introduction to Data Science

Aditi and Arjun began by discussing the core principles of data science. They revisited the data science lifecycle, which includes data collection, data cleaning, data analysis, and data visualization. They reviewed the importance of each phase and how it contributes to deriving actionable insights.

Arjun: "The data science lifecycle is like a roadmap. Each step is crucial for transforming raw data into meaningful insights."

Aditi: "Exactly. Data collection and cleaning set the stage for analysis. Without clean data, our results won't be reliable."

They then moved on to review the basic statistics necessary for data analysis, including measures of central tendency (mean, median, mode) and measures of dispersion (range, variance, standard deviation).

Day 2-4: Data Wrangling and EDA

Data wrangling and exploratory data analysis were the focus for the next few days. They worked on real datasets, practicing techniques for cleaning and preparing data for analysis. They discussed methods for handling missing values, outliers, and data inconsistencies.

Aditi: "Handling missing data is always a challenge. I usually start with imputation methods, but sometimes it's better to remove certain rows or columns."

Arjun: "Agreed. It depends on the dataset and the analysis we're conducting. I find visualizing the data helps in identifying patterns and anomalies."

They also explored EDA techniques, including plotting histograms, box plots, and scatter plots to understand the distribution and relationships within the data.

Day 5-7: Machine Learning Algorithms

The focus then shifted to machine learning algorithms. They reviewed both supervised and unsupervised learning methods. They began with linear regression and classification algorithms, discussing their applications and limitations.

Arjun: "Linear regression is straightforward but powerful. It's great for understanding relationships between variables."

Aditi: "For classification, I've always been intrigued by decision trees. They're easy to interpret and useful for complex datasets."

They implemented simple algorithms using libraries like Scikit-Learn and observed how different models performed on sample datasets.

Day 8-10: Model Evaluation

Understanding how to evaluate the performance of machine learning models was crucial. They delved into metrics such as accuracy, precision, recall, and F1 score for classification models, and Mean Absolute Error (MAE) and R-squared for regression models.

Aditi: "Evaluating models is where the real work begins. Accuracy alone isn't enough; we need to consider other metrics depending on the problem."

Arjun: "True. For imbalanced datasets, metrics like precision and recall become more important than overall accuracy."

3. Day 11-30: Intermediate Concepts

As they progressed, the focus shifted to more intermediate concepts, including feature engineering, model selection, and hyperparameter tuning.

Day 11-15: Feature Engineering

Feature engineering was a critical area of focus. They discussed techniques for creating new features from existing data, such as polynomial features, interaction terms, and dimensionality reduction methods like PCA (Principal Component Analysis).

Arjun: "Feature engineering can really make a difference in model performance. Sometimes, a well-engineered feature can significantly improve results."

Aditi: "Yes, and dimensionality reduction helps in simplifying models and reducing overfitting. PCA is a powerful tool for that."

They practiced feature engineering on various datasets, experimenting with different techniques and evaluating their impact on model performance.

Day 16-20: Model Selection and Validation

Model selection and validation were next. They reviewed methods for splitting data into training and testing sets, cross-validation techniques, and how to choose the best model based on performance metrics.

Aditi: "Cross-validation helps in assessing how well our model generalizes to unseen data. It's essential for avoiding overfitting."

Arjun: "Exactly. And model selection involves comparing different algorithms and choosing the one that best suits the problem at hand."

They applied these techniques to their own projects, selecting models and validating their performance using various methods.

Day 21-30: Advanced Machine Learning

The final days of this phase were devoted to advanced machine learning topics, including ensemble methods, neural networks, and deep learning. They explored algorithms like Random Forests, Gradient Boosting, and basic neural network architectures.

Arjun: "Ensemble methods like Random Forests combine multiple models to improve performance. They're particularly useful for complex datasets."

Aditi: "Neural networks are fascinating, especially with deep learning. They've revolutionized many fields, but they also require careful tuning."

They implemented and tested these advanced techniques on more complex datasets, gaining hands-on experience with cutting-edge methods.

4. Day 31-60: Applied Data Science

In the second half of their journey, Aditi and Arjun applied their knowledge to real-world problems and projects. They worked on a series of mini-projects, each designed to reinforce their learning and challenge their skills.

Day 31-40: Project 1 - Predictive Modeling

Their first project involved building a predictive model to forecast sales for a retail company. They applied everything from data wrangling to model evaluation, focusing on practical implementation.

Aditi: "For this project, we need to ensure that our features are relevant and that our model is robust. Let's start by exploring the data thoroughly."

Arjun: "Agreed. We'll use techniques like feature scaling and regularization to enhance our model's performance."

They built and evaluated various models, including linear regression and Random Forests, refining their approach based on performance metrics.

Day 41-50: Project 2 - Classification Challenge

Their next project was a classification challenge involving customer segmentation for targeted marketing. They used clustering techniques and classification algorithms to group customers and predict their behaviors.

Arjun: "Clustering can help us identify distinct customer segments. We should use algorithms like K-Means and evaluate the results with silhouette scores."

Aditi: "For classification, we'll need to carefully tune our models and validate them using cross-validation to ensure accuracy."

They explored different clustering and classification methods, analyzing the results to refine their approach.

Day 51-60: Project 3 - Time Series Analysis

Their final project focused on time series analysis, predicting stock prices using historical data. They applied techniques like ARIMA models and LSTM networks, gaining experience with time-dependent data.

Aditi: "Time series analysis requires special consideration of trends and seasonality. Let's start with ARIMA and then move to more complex models like LSTM."

Arjun: "Absolutely. We need to preprocess the data effectively and evaluate our models with appropriate metrics for time series."

They implemented and tested different time series models, analyzing their predictions and assessing their accuracy.

5. Day 61-75: Consolidation and Reflection

The final phase of their journey was dedicated to consolidating their learning and reflecting on their progress. They revisited key concepts, reviewed their projects, and discussed how their skills had evolved.

Day 61-65: Review and Reinforcement

Aditi and Arjun reviewed the concepts they had covered, reinforcing their understanding through discussions and additional exercises. They revisited challenging topics and clarified any remaining doubts.

Arjun: "Reviewing our past work helps us see how much we've learned and where we can still improve."

Aditi: "It's also an opportunity to consolidate our knowledge and ensure that we're comfortable with all the concepts we've covered."

They conducted mock interviews and practiced explaining their projects, preparing for real-world applications and potential job interviews.

Day 66-75: Future Directions and Goals

In the final days, Aditi and Arjun discussed their future goals and how they could continue to advance their data science skills. They explored emerging trends and technologies, setting new objectives for their professional development.

Aditi: "Our journey has been incredibly rewarding. We've gained a lot of practical experience and deepened our understanding of data science."

Arjun: "I agree. Looking ahead, we should focus on staying updated with new developments and exploring areas like AI ethics and explainability."

They set goals for continuing their education, attending conferences, and contributing to open-source projects. Their shared passion for data science had become a driving force in their relationship, and they were excited to continue exploring the field together.

6. Conclusion

As their structured learning journey concluded, Aditi and Arjun reflected on the growth they had experienced both individually and as a team. Their deep dive into data science had not only enhanced their professional skills but also strengthened their bond. The challenges they faced and overcame together had deepened their connection and solidified their partnership.

Their journey through data science had been a testament to their commitment to learning and to each other. It had reinforced their shared values of collaboration, curiosity, and perseverance. With a solid foundation and a shared vision for the future, Aditi and Arjun were ready to tackle new challenges and continue their exploration of data science, both in their careers and in their lives together.

In this chapter, Aditi and Arjun's structured learning journey through data science highlights their commitment to professional growth and their collaborative spirit. The chapter captures their daily interactions, discussions, and challenges as they tackle fundamental and advanced concepts. Through their shared learning experience, they not only enhance their data science skills but also strengthen their relationship, demonstrating the power of collaboration and mutual support in achieving personal and professional goals.

Chapter 8: Day wise Love and Learning

In the world of data science, where algorithms and models reign supreme, Aditi and Arjun embarked on a journey that combined their love for each other with their passion for learning. For the next 75 days, they would explore the depths of data science, intertwining their personal connection with their professional growth. Each day was carefully planned, not only to enhance their understanding of data science but also to deepen their bond. This chapter chronicles their unique learning adventure, filled with romance, discovery, and the joy of shared knowledge.

Day 1-10: Basics of Data Science

Day 1: Introduction to Statistics

Their journey began with a discussion on statistics, the foundation of data science. They started by revisiting fundamental concepts like mean, median, mode, and standard deviation. To make the session more engaging, Arjun set up a fun experiment.

Arjun: "Let's analyze the statistics of our favorite movies. We'll calculate the average rating and the standard deviation for each genre."

Aditi: "Sounds great! I'll gather the data while you prepare the analysis."

As they worked through the data, their conversation flowed seamlessly between statistical formulas and their favorite films. The task became a blend of learning and personal bonding.

Day 2: Probability and Distributions

The focus shifted to probability theory and different types of distributions. They discussed the normal distribution, binomial distribution, and the concept of statistical significance.

Aditi: "Understanding distributions is crucial for making sense of data. It's like understanding the rules of a game before you play."

Arjun: "Exactly. And probability helps us gauge the likelihood of events. It's foundational for making predictions."

They illustrated these concepts with practical examples, such as predicting the likelihood of certain events happening in their daily lives, which added a playful element to their learning.

Day 3-4: Data Cleaning

Data cleaning was the next step. They tackled real-world datasets, identifying and handling missing values, outliers, and inconsistencies.

Aditi: "Cleaning data is like preparing ingredients for a recipe. If the ingredients aren't right, the final dish won't turn out well."

Arjun: "I agree. Let's use this dataset to practice different cleaning techniques and see how they affect our results."

They spent time cleaning and analyzing the data together, turning a technical task into a collaborative and insightful experience.

Day 5-7: Exploratory Data Analysis (EDA)

Exploratory Data Analysis was a pivotal topic. They used visualizations like histograms, box plots, and scatter plots to understand the data better.

Arjun: "EDA is about uncovering the story behind the data. It's like detective work."

Aditi: "And visualizations make the story clearer. Let's create some plots and see what insights we can uncover."

Their EDA sessions were marked by discoveries and discussions about the data's patterns and trends, which often led to deeper conversations about their own experiences and perspectives.

Day 8-10: Data Preparation and Feature Engineering

The final days of the basics covered data preparation and feature engineering. They discussed how to select and transform features to improve model performance.

Aditi: "Feature engineering is where creativity meets data science. We can engineer new features to capture more information."

Arjun: "Yes, and it's crucial for building effective models. Let's try creating some new features and see how they impact our analysis."

Their feature engineering exercises were accompanied by brainstorming sessions about real-world applications, blending technical skills with creative thinking.

Day 11-20: Introduction to Machine Learning

Day 11: Overview of Machine Learning

They began their exploration of machine learning by differentiating between supervised and unsupervised learning. They discussed various algorithms and their applications.

Aditi: "Supervised learning uses labeled data to train models, while unsupervised learning finds patterns in unlabeled data."

Arjun: "Exactly. Let's start with a simple supervised learning algorithm and see how it performs on a dataset."

They implemented basic algorithms like linear regression and k-means clustering, using practical examples to illustrate their concepts.

Day 12-14: Linear Regression and Classification

They delved deeper into linear regression and classification algorithms, discussing their applications and limitations.

Arjun: "Linear regression is great for understanding relationships between variables, while classification helps us categorize data into different classes."

Aditi: "Let's apply these algorithms to a real dataset and compare their performance. We can also explore metrics like accuracy and precision."

Their hands-on approach to implementing and evaluating models provided them with practical insights and fostered engaging discussions.

Day 15-17: Unsupervised Learning and Clustering

Unsupervised learning and clustering algorithms were the next focus. They explored k-means clustering and hierarchical clustering, discussing their use cases and implementation.

Aditi: "Unsupervised learning is fascinating because it finds patterns in data without predefined labels."

Arjun: "Clustering helps us group similar data points together. Let's experiment with different clustering methods and see what insights we can uncover."

Their clustering exercises led to intriguing findings and discussions about the implications of their results.

Day 18-20: Dimensionality Reduction

The final days of this phase covered dimensionality reduction techniques like Principal Component Analysis (PCA). They discussed how reducing the number of features can simplify models and improve performance.

Arjun: "Dimensionality reduction is like simplifying a complex story into key points. It helps us focus on the most important information."

Aditi: "Yes, and PCA is a powerful tool for achieving that. Let's apply PCA to our dataset and analyze the results."

Their exploration of dimensionality reduction techniques demonstrated the importance of simplifying data while retaining essential information.

Day 21-30: Advanced Algorithms

Day 21: Introduction to Advanced Algorithms

They began exploring advanced algorithms, including Support Vector Machines (SVM) and Decision Trees. They discussed how these algorithms work and their advantages.

Aditi: "SVM is great for classification tasks, especially with complex boundaries. Decision Trees are intuitive and easy to interpret."

Arjun: "Exactly. Let's implement these algorithms and compare their performance on a classification problem."

Their implementation of SVM and Decision Trees provided them with deeper insights into model complexity and performance.

Day 22-25: Neural Networks and Deep Learning Basics

The focus shifted to neural networks and deep learning. They discussed the architecture of neural networks, including layers, activation functions, and backpropagation.

Arjun: "Neural networks mimic the human brain, with layers of interconnected nodes. They're powerful for learning complex patterns."

Aditi: "Yes, and deep learning takes it further with more layers. Let's build a simple neural network and observe how it learns."

Their hands-on work with neural networks led to discussions about the power and limitations of deep learning models.

Day 26-30: Support Vector Machines and Decision Trees

They revisited Support Vector Machines and Decision Trees, applying them to more complex datasets and exploring their performance.

Aditi: "Support Vector Machines are effective in high-dimensional spaces. Decision Trees, on the other hand, are great for interpretability."

Arjun: "Let's compare their performance on different datasets and discuss their strengths and weaknesses."

Their in-depth analysis of these algorithms provided them with a comprehensive understanding of their applications and limitations.

Day 31-40: Model Evaluation

Day 31: Cross-Validation and Model Selection

They began their exploration of model evaluation with cross-validation techniques, discussing how to assess model performance and prevent overfitting.

Arjun: "Cross-validation helps us evaluate how well our model generalizes to unseen data. It's essential for reliable performance."

Aditi: "Yes, and it's important to use different techniques like k-fold cross-validation to get a robust estimate."

Their practical exercises in cross-validation and model selection led to discussions about the importance of model evaluation in real-world applications.

Day 32-35: ROC Curves and AUC

They explored ROC curves and the Area Under the Curve (AUC) as metrics for evaluating classification models. They discussed how these metrics help in assessing model performance.

Aditi: "ROC curves provide a visual representation of a model's performance across different thresholds. AUC quantifies the overall ability of the model."

Arjun: "Exactly. Let's generate ROC curves for our models and compare their AUC scores."

Their analysis of ROC curves and AUC scores provided them with valuable insights into model performance and trade-offs.

Day 36-40: Precision-Recall and Evaluation Metrics

The final days of this phase covered precision-recall metrics, discussing their importance for evaluating models, especially in imbalanced datasets.

Arjun: "Precision and recall are crucial for evaluating models in scenarios where class distribution is uneven."

Aditi: "Yes, and the F1 score balances precision and recall. Let's calculate these metrics for our models and discuss their implications."

Their evaluation of precision-recall metrics led to discussions about the challenges of working with imbalanced datasets and strategies for addressing them.

Day 41-50: Data Engineering

Day 41: Introduction to Data Engineering

They began their exploration of data engineering, discussing the importance of data pipelines, ETL (Extract, Transform, Load) processes, and big data tools.

Aditi: "Data engineering is about building the infrastructure for data collection, processing, and analysis. It's essential for handling large-scale data."

Arjun: "Exactly. Let's explore some big data tools and see how they fit into the data engineering process."

Their exploration of data engineering concepts provided them with a deeper understanding of the infrastructure required for data science.

Day 42-45: Feature Engineering and Transformation

The focus shifted to feature engineering and transformation techniques. They discussed methods for creating and transforming features to improve model performance.

Arjun: "Feature engineering is like adding new ingredients to a recipe to enhance its flavor. It can significantly impact model performance."

Aditi: "Yes, and feature transformation techniques like scaling and normalization help in making features more comparable."

Their hands-on work with feature engineering and transformation techniques demonstrated their impact on model performance.

Day 46-50: Big Data Tools and Frameworks

They explored big data tools and frameworks like Hadoop and Spark, discussing their applications and advantages for handling large datasets.

Aditi: "Hadoop and Spark are powerful tools for processing large-scale data. They allow us to perform distributed computing and handle massive datasets."

Arjun: "Exactly. Let's look into how these tools work and their practical applications in data engineering."

Their exploration of big data tools provided them with insights into handling large-scale data and the challenges associated with it.

Day 51-60: Deep Learning

Day 51: Introduction to Deep Learning

They began their deep learning journey by exploring the basics of Convolutional Neural Networks (CNNs) and their applications in image processing.

Arjun: "CNNs are designed to process grid-like data, such as images. They use convolutional layers to extract features and perform classification."

Aditi: "Yes, and they've revolutionized image recognition tasks. Let's build a simple CNN and see how it performs on an image dataset."

Their hands-on work with CNNs provided them with practical experience in building and evaluating deep learning models.

Day 52-55: Recurrent Neural Networks (RNNs)

The focus shifted to Recurrent Neural Networks (RNNs) and their applications in sequential data analysis, such as time series and natural language processing.

Aditi: "RNNs are designed to handle sequential data by maintaining a state over time. They're great for tasks like language modeling and time series prediction."

Arjun: "Exactly. Let's build an RNN model and apply it to a sequence prediction problem."

Their exploration of RNNs led to discussions about the challenges of working with sequential data and strategies for addressing them.

Day 56-60: Transformers and Attention Mechanisms

The final days of this phase covered Transformers and attention mechanisms, discussing their impact on natural language processing tasks.

Arjun: *"Transformers have revolutionized NLP with their attention mechanisms, allowing models to focus on different parts of the input sequence."*

Aditi: *"Yes, and models like BERT and GPT have set new standards in NLP. Let's explore how Transformers work and their applications."*

Their exploration of Transformers provided them with insights into cutting-edge techniques in deep learning and natural language processing.

Day 61-70: Practical Applications

Day 61: Natural Language Processing (NLP)

They began their exploration of NLP by discussing text processing techniques, including tokenization, stemming, and lemmatization.

Aditi: *"NLP involves processing and analyzing textual data. Techniques like tokenization help us break down text into manageable pieces."*

Arjun: *"Exactly. Let's apply these techniques to a text dataset and explore methods for text classification and sentiment analysis."*

Their hands-on work with NLP techniques provided them with practical experience in processing and analyzing textual data.

Day 62-65: Computer Vision

The focus shifted to computer vision, discussing techniques for image processing, object detection, and image classification.

Arjun: "Computer vision allows us to extract information from images. Techniques like object detection and image classification are essential for various applications."

Aditi: "Yes, and CNNs are particularly effective for computer vision tasks. Let's implement some image processing techniques and explore their results."

Their exploration of computer vision techniques provided them with insights into analyzing and interpreting visual data.

Day 66-70: AI Ethics and Responsible AI

The final days of this phase covered AI ethics and responsible AI practices, discussing the ethical implications of AI technologies and the importance of fairness and transparency.

Aditi: "AI ethics is crucial for ensuring that our models and systems are fair and unbiased. We need to consider the social impact of our work."

Arjun: "Exactly. Responsible AI practices help us build systems that are ethical and transparent. Let's discuss some case studies and ethical considerations."

Their discussions on AI ethics provided them with a deeper understanding of the responsibility associated with developing and deploying AI technologies.

Day 71-75: Interview Preparation and Mock Interviews

Day 71-72: Review of Key Concepts

They began their interview preparation by reviewing key concepts and revisiting the topics they had covered during their learning journey.

Arjun: "It's important to review our key concepts and make sure we're comfortable with the material. Let's go over some of the topics we found challenging."

Aditi: "Yes, and we should also practice explaining these concepts clearly. It's essential for performing well in interviews."

Their review sessions helped them consolidate their knowledge and prepare for interview questions.

Day 73-74: Mock Interviews

They conducted mock interviews to simulate real-world interview scenarios. They prepared questions based on their learning journey and provided feedback to each other.

Aditi: "Let's conduct a mock interview session. I'll ask you some technical questions, and we can discuss your answers and areas for improvement."

Arjun: "Great idea. I'll also prepare some questions for you. This will help us practice and refine our interview skills."

Their mock interviews provided them with valuable experience and feedback, helping them feel more confident and prepared.

Day 75: Final Reflections and Future Goals

On the final day, they reflected on their learning journey and discussed their future goals.

Aditi: "This journey has been incredible. We've learned so much and grown both personally and professionally."

Arjun: "I agree. We've faced challenges and achieved milestones together. Let's set new goals for our future and continue exploring data science."

Their reflections marked the end of their 75-day learning adventure, highlighting the personal and professional growth they had experienced.

Conclusion

Aditi and Arjun's 75-day journey through data science was more than just a learning experience; it was a testament to their commitment to each other and their shared passion for knowledge. Each day of their structured learning adventure blended romance and education, fostering a deeper connection and enhancing their professional skills. Their journey through data science not only strengthened their bond but also prepared them for future challenges and opportunities. With a solid foundation in data science and a renewed sense of purpose, Aditi and Arjun were ready to tackle new horizons, both in their careers and in their lives together.

Chapter 9: The Interview

Aditi and Arjun had spent the last 75 days delving into the world of data science, seamlessly blending their professional growth with their personal connection. With their interview dates fast approaching, the final chapter of their preparation journey was upon them. This chapter focuses on the critical period leading up to their interviews, capturing their preparation, the emotional stakes, and their ultimate success.

Morning of Preparation

The sun had barely risen when Aditi and Arjun, both clad in their respective comfy but professional attire, sat down at their shared workspace. The room was filled with the hum of computers, scattered notes, and the aroma of freshly brewed coffee. Today was a pivotal day for both of them—final preparation for their interviews. They had set aside this day to consolidate their knowledge, practice answering questions, and fine-tune their strategies.

Arjun: "Alright, let's start by reviewing our key concepts. I'll begin with machine learning algorithms and their applications. We need to be ready to discuss everything from linear regression to deep learning."

Aditi: "Sounds good. I'll take care of the model evaluation metrics and the practical applications we've studied. We should also go through some recent case studies and industry trends."

As they dived into their preparation, they alternated between discussing technical topics, solving problems, and quizzing each other on key concepts. Their interactions were a blend of intense focus and light-hearted banter, reflecting their well-established rapport.

Mock Interviews

By mid-afternoon, they decided to conduct mock interviews to simulate real-world scenarios. They had set up a mock interview environment, complete with a timer and a list of potential questions.

Aditi: "I'll start as the interviewer. Here's your first question: Explain the concept of overfitting and how you would address it in a machine learning model."

Arjun: "Overfitting occurs when a model learns the training data too well, capturing noise and resulting in poor performance on unseen data. To address overfitting, we can use techniques such as cross-validation, regularization, and pruning decision trees."

Aditi: "That's a good explanation. Now, let's move on to a more complex question: How would you handle an imbalanced dataset in a classification problem?"

Arjun: "For imbalanced datasets, we can use techniques such as resampling (oversampling the minority class or undersampling the majority class), synthetic data generation (like SMOTE), or adjusting class weights in the model."

As they practiced, they provided each other with constructive feedback. Aditi noted Arjun's ability to explain complex concepts clearly, while Arjun appreciated Aditi's analytical approach to problem-solving. Their mock interviews not only prepared them for potential questions but also highlighted areas where they needed improvement.

Review and Reflection

As the evening approached, they took a break to reflect on their progress and review their preparation. They sat in the living room, surrounded by textbooks and notebooks, discussing their thoughts and strategies.

Aditi: "I feel confident about the technical questions, but I'm also thinking about how to handle behavioral questions. It's important to convey our teamwork and problem-solving skills effectively."

Arjun: "Absolutely. Let's go over some common behavioral questions. We should be ready to discuss our past experiences and how we've applied our skills in real-world scenarios."

They revisited their past projects and experiences, crafting stories that showcased their skills and achievements. They practiced articulating their experiences in a way that highlighted their strengths and demonstrated their suitability for the roles they were applying for.

The Day of the Interview

The day of the interviews arrived with a mixture of excitement and nerves. Aditi and Arjun had agreed to spend the morning separately, giving each other space to prepare mentally. They met up in the afternoon to offer final words of encouragement before heading to their respective interview locations.

Aditi: "We've prepared well. Just remember to stay calm, be clear, and showcase your passion for data science. You'll do great."

Arjun: "Thanks, Aditi. You too. We've got this."

They embraced, a gesture that symbolized their support for each other. With a final look of reassurance, they parted ways, each heading to their interview.

Arjun's Interview

Arjun arrived at the tech company's office, greeted by a sleek modern design and a bustling atmosphere. He was escorted to a conference room where his interview was set to take place. The interview panel consisted of two senior data scientists who began with technical questions.

Interviewer 1: "Can you walk us through a recent project where you applied machine learning techniques?"

Arjun: "Certainly. In my recent project, I worked on predicting customer churn using a combination of logistic regression and decision trees. We focused on feature engineering to improve model accuracy and used cross-validation to ensure robustness."

As the interview progressed, Arjun demonstrated his deep understanding of data science concepts, providing detailed explanations and showcasing his problem-solving skills. He handled behavioral questions with confidence, sharing stories of teamwork and overcoming challenges.

Interviewer 2: "How do you stay updated with the latest trends in data science?"

Arjun: "I regularly follow industry blogs, attend conferences, and participate in online courses. Staying updated is crucial for adapting to new technologies and methodologies."

The interview concluded with a discussion of Arjun's questions about the role and the company. He left the office feeling a sense of accomplishment and optimism.

Aditi's Interview

Aditi arrived at her interview location, a prestigious research institute known for its cutting-edge work in AI. The atmosphere was calm and professional, and she was soon ushered into the interview room where she met with a panel of researchers.

Interviewer 1: "Tell us about your experience with neural networks and their applications."

Aditi: "In my recent work, I developed a convolutional neural network for image classification. We used transfer learning to leverage pre-trained models and fine-tuned them for our specific dataset."

Throughout the interview, Aditi showcased her technical expertise and her ability to communicate complex ideas effectively. She was also asked about her approach to problem-solving and her experience working on collaborative projects.

Interviewer 2: "Can you give an example of a challenging problem you faced and how you resolved it?"

Aditi: "Certainly. One of the challenges I faced was dealing with a noisy dataset. I implemented various data cleaning techniques and used feature selection to improve model performance. The result was a more robust model that met our project goals."

Aditi's interview concluded with a discussion of her long-term career goals and how they aligned with the institute's mission. She left the interview feeling satisfied and hopeful.

Post-Interview Reflections

After their interviews, Aditi and Arjun reconvened at their shared workspace. They exchanged their experiences and reflected on the process.

Aditi: *"The interviews went well. I felt confident answering the technical questions and discussing my experiences. How about you?"*

Arjun: *"I felt the same. The technical questions were challenging, but I was able to showcase my skills. I'm optimistic about the outcome."*

They spent the evening celebrating their achievements, reflecting on their journey, and discussing their future plans. Their successful interviews were a testament to their hard work, dedication, and the support they had provided each other.

Conclusion

Chapter 9 marks the culmination of Aditi and Arjun's 75-day learning journey. Their interviews were not just a test of their technical skills but also a reflection of their commitment to each other and their shared passion for data science. The chapter captures the essence of their preparation, the challenges they faced, and their ultimate success. As they looked forward to new opportunities and continued their journey together, their experiences served as a reminder of their growth and the power of collaboration and mutual support.

Chapter 10: The Union

The Results

The email notifications arrived simultaneously, marking a significant milestone in Aditi and Arjun's lives. Both had awaited this moment with bated breath. After weeks of preparation, countless hours of study, and the emotional rollercoaster of interviews, the results were in.

Aditi's inbox pinged first. She clicked on the subject line, "Congratulations from [Institute Name]." Her heart raced as she read through the email, absorbing the words: "We are pleased to offer you the position of Senior Data Scientist at [Institute Name]. Your interview demonstrated an exceptional understanding of advanced data science concepts and a strong fit with our team's goals."

A smile spread across her face. She quickly typed a message to Arjun: "I got the job! Can't wait to hear about yours."

Arjun's phone buzzed moments later. His email was from the tech company where he had interviewed. The subject read, "Offer of Employment." He clicked eagerly and read the message: "We are excited to extend an offer for the position of Data Scientist at [Tech Company]. Your technical skills and problem-solving abilities impressed us greatly."

He exhaled deeply, a sense of accomplishment washing over him. He immediately replied to Aditi's message: "I got the offer too! This is incredible!"

Celebration

They decided to celebrate their successes together. They met at their favorite café, a cozy place where they had spent countless hours discussing algorithms, data science theories, and their personal lives. This time, however, the conversation was filled with excitement about their new roles and the journey that lay ahead.

Arjun: "Can you believe it? We both did it!"

Aditi: "It feels surreal. We've worked so hard for this. It's amazing to see our efforts pay off."

They clinked their coffee cups, a symbolic gesture of their joint victory. The café was bustling with energy, but their corner table felt like a world of its own, filled with shared memories and dreams.

Arjun: "I'm really proud of how we supported each other throughout this journey. It made all the difference."

Aditi: "Absolutely. And our collaboration on the data science project was a huge part of this success. We really complemented each other's strengths."

Reconciliation

Their celebration continued with a walk through the nearby park, where they reminisced about their past misunderstandings. The silence and confusion that had once seemed insurmountable now felt like a distant memory, overshadowed by their shared triumphs and the deeper understanding they had developed.

Aditi: "I've been thinking about our misunderstandings. It's clear now how much we've grown from those experiences."

Arjun: "Yes, and it was through those challenges that we learned how to communicate better and support each other more effectively. I'm grateful for that."

They sat on a bench, enjoying the tranquility of the park and reflecting on their journey. The shared experience of overcoming obstacles had only strengthened their bond.

Arjun: "I realize now that our misunderstandings were a part of our growth. They helped us understand each other on a deeper level."

Aditi: "I agree. And now, we're stronger for it. We've learned how to navigate challenges together and come out even more united."

Looking Forward

As the evening approached, they decided to discuss their future together. With their professional achievements in hand, they were eager to envision what lay ahead.

Aditi: "So, what's next for us? We have new roles and new challenges, but what about our personal goals?"

Arjun: "I think we should continue building on what we've achieved. Let's set new goals, both professionally and personally. We've proven that we can accomplish great things together."

Aditi: "I like that idea. We can use our experiences to drive our future projects and also focus on our personal growth. Maybe even explore new hobbies or interests together."

They discussed their aspirations, from advancing in their careers to pursuing personal interests. Their plans included traveling, taking on new projects, and continuing their mutual support for each other's goals.

Arjun: "And let's not forget to keep learning and growing. Our journey in data science has been incredibly fulfilling, and I'm excited about the new challenges and opportunities ahead."

Aditi: "Definitely. We've proven that we can achieve great things together. Let's make the most of every opportunity and keep supporting each other along the way."

A New Beginning

As the sun set, painting the sky with hues of orange and pink, Aditi and Arjun stood hand in hand, ready to embrace their future. Their professional achievements had brought them closer, and their journey together had been a testament to their resilience, dedication, and love.

Aditi: *"Here's to our future and all the adventures it will bring."*

Arjun: *"To our future, and to the strength of our partnership. I'm excited about what lies ahead."*

They shared a warm embrace, their hearts full of hope and anticipation. Their journey was far from over, but with their shared achievements and strengthened bond, they felt ready to face whatever came next.

Conclusion

Chapter 10 captures the essence of Aditi and Arjun's journey from professional success to personal fulfillment. Their successful interviews marked a new chapter in their lives, symbolizing not just career achievements but also a deeper understanding and connection between them. Their reconciliation of past misunderstandings and their focus on future goals exemplified the strength of their relationship and their commitment to each other. As they looked forward to a future filled with opportunities and shared dreams, their story was a testament to the power of love, support, and the pursuit of excellence.

Chapter 11: Khamoshi Revisited

A Time for Reflection

The sun had dipped below the horizon, casting a gentle twilight over the city. Aditi and Arjun were settled in their favorite corner of the living room, surrounded by the comfort of their home. Their journey had been a remarkable one, full of triumphs and trials, love and learning. As they prepared to wind down from a busy day, they decided it was time to reflect on their journey and the role that silence had played in their relationship.

Arjun: "It's incredible to think about where we started and where we are now. I can't help but reflect on how significant the silence was in our journey."

Aditi: "I've been thinking about that too. The period of silence was tough, but it taught us so much about communication, patience, and understanding. It was a turning point in our relationship."

Arjun: "Yes, the silence allowed us to reassess and grow individually. It made us appreciate the value of open communication and the importance of addressing misunderstandings early on."

As they reminisced, they found themselves revisiting the silence that had once created a chasm between them. What had initially felt like an insurmountable barrier had, in reality, been a profound period of growth.

The Significance of Silence

Their period of silence had been a complex and emotional time. What had begun as a misunderstanding over project deadlines had evolved into a profound silence that lasted two weeks. During this time, both had faced internal struggles and reflections, each grappling with their own emotions and thoughts.

Aditi: "I remember feeling a deep sense of confusion and frustration during those two weeks. I didn't know how to reach out, and I think we both needed that space to process our feelings."

Arjun: "Absolutely. The silence gave us the opportunity to reflect on our priorities and understand what we truly wanted, both professionally and personally. It was a challenging period, but it was also a time of significant self-discovery."

Their silence had not been merely an absence of communication but a time of introspection. It allowed them to confront their individual fears and aspirations, ultimately leading to a deeper understanding of themselves and each other.

Aditi: "One of the biggest lessons I learned was the importance of addressing issues before they escalate. We both needed to communicate our concerns openly rather than letting them build up."

Arjun: "And I learned the value of patience and empathy. Sometimes, taking a step back allows us to see things more clearly and approach the situation with a more balanced perspective."

Growth Through Adversity

The silence had been a catalyst for change in their relationship. It had pushed them to confront their assumptions and strengthen their communication skills. The lessons learned during this period had become integral to their relationship moving forward.

Aditi: "The way we handled that silence made us stronger as a couple. It showed us that we could navigate difficult times and emerge with a better understanding of each other."

Arjun: "Yes, and it also highlighted the importance of mutual support. Even when we weren't speaking, we were still thinking about each other and our relationship. It reinforced our commitment to each other."

Their growth during the silence was not just about overcoming challenges but also about appreciating the strength of their bond. It had deepened their connection and made them more resilient in the face of future challenges.

Blending Love and Career

As they moved past the period of silence, Aditi and Arjun found that their personal and professional lives were intertwined in meaningful ways. Their shared passion for data science had brought them closer, and their achievements had strengthened their bond.

Aditi: "Our journey in data science has been a significant part of our story. It's amazing how our professional achievements have complemented our personal growth."

Arjun: "Indeed. Our shared projects and learning experiences have not only enhanced our careers but also brought us closer together. We've learned to balance our professional ambitions with our personal relationship."

Their ability to blend their love for data science with their relationship had been a unique aspect of their journey. They had managed to find harmony between their careers and their personal lives, using their shared goals as a foundation for their relationship.

Aditi: "I think our shared interests have helped us understand each other on a deeper level. It's not just about working together but also about sharing our passions and dreams."

Arjun: "Exactly. Our relationship is built on mutual respect and shared goals. It's been incredible to see how our personal and professional lives intersect and support each other."

Their shared journey in data science had been more than just a professional endeavor; it had been a source of inspiration and growth in their personal lives. It had allowed them to support each other's ambitions while building a strong foundation for their future together.

Commitment to Each Other

As they looked towards the future, Aditi and Arjun felt a renewed sense of commitment to each other. Their journey had taught them valuable lessons about love, communication, and resilience. They were ready to embrace the future with confidence, knowing that they had built a strong and supportive relationship.

Aditi: "Looking back on our journey, I feel incredibly grateful for what we've accomplished together. We've faced challenges, celebrated successes, and grown so much as a couple."

Arjun: "I feel the same way. Our journey has been full of lessons and achievements. I'm excited about what the future holds for us, both personally and professionally."

They made a pact to continue supporting each other, both in their careers and in their personal lives. Their commitment was a reflection of their shared values and aspirations.

Aditi: "Let's make a promise to keep growing together, to support each other's dreams, and to navigate any challenges that come our way."

Arjun: "I promise to always be there for you, to communicate openly, and to continue building a future together that we both envision."

Their commitment was not just a promise but a reflection of their shared journey and the deep connection they had forged. It was a commitment to continue learning, growing, and supporting each other as they faced new challenges and opportunities.

A New Chapter

As the night settled around them, Aditi and Arjun looked forward to a new chapter in their lives. Their journey had been a testament to their resilience, love, and dedication. They had navigated the complexities of their professional and personal lives, emerging stronger and more united.

Aditi: "Here's to a future filled with continued growth, love, and shared dreams."

Arjun: "To our future, and to the strength of our bond. I'm excited about what lies ahead and grateful for everything we've accomplished together."

They embraced, a gesture that symbolized their commitment to each other and their shared future. As they looked out at the city lights, they felt a sense of anticipation and hope for the journey ahead.

Conclusion

Chapter 11 encapsulates the essence of Aditi and Arjun's journey, reflecting on the significance of their period of silence and the lessons learned. Their ability to blend love and career, their commitment to each other, and their shared dreams were the cornerstones of their relationship. As they looked forward to a future filled with opportunities and challenges, they were prepared to face it together, with a renewed sense of purpose and a deepened bond. Their story was a testament to the power of love, resilience, and the ability to navigate life's complexities together.

Interview Guide: Basics of Statistics and Probability

Introduction

In the realm of data science and analytics, a strong foundation in statistics and probability is essential. This guide provides a clear and easy-to-understand overview of fundamental concepts, including measures of central tendency, measures of variability, and probability distributions. By mastering these basics, you'll be better prepared for interviews and real-world data analysis tasks.

---

1. Statistics & Probability Basics

1.1 Measures of Central Tendency

Mean: The mean, often referred to as the average, is calculated by summing all the values in a dataset and dividing by the number of values. It provides a measure of the central value of the dataset.

Formula: Mean=Σxin\text{Mean} = \frac{\sum x_i}{n}Mean=nΣxi where Σxi\sum x_iΣxi is the sum of all values and nnn is the number of values.

Example: Consider the dataset: 2, 4, 6, 8, 10. Mean=2+4+6+8+105=305=6\text{Mean} = \frac{2 + 4 + 6 + 8 + 10}{5} = \frac{30}{5} = 6Mean=52+4+6+8+10=530=6

Median: The median is the middle value in a dataset when the values are arranged in ascending or descending order. If there's an even number of observations, the median is the average of the two middle numbers.

Steps:

1. Sort the data.
2. Find the middle value (or the average of the two middle values if there is an even number of observations).

Example: For the dataset 2, 4, 6, 8, 10 (odd number of values): Median = 6.

For the dataset 1, 3, 5, 7 (even number of values): Median = $\frac{3+5}{2} = 4$.

Mode: The mode is the value that appears most frequently in a dataset. A dataset may have one mode, more than one mode, or no mode if no number repeats.

Example: In the dataset 2, 3, 3, 4, 5, the mode is 3, as it appears most frequently.

1.2 Measures of Variability

Standard Deviation: The standard deviation measures the dispersion or spread of a dataset. It quantifies how much the values deviate from the mean.

Formula:
$$\text{Standard Deviation} = \sqrt{\frac{\sum (x_i - \text{mean})^2}{n}}$$

where x_i represents each value, and mean is the mean of the dataset.

Example: For the dataset 2, 4, 6, 8, 10:

1. Mean = 6

2. Variance = $\frac{(2-6)^2 + (4-6)^2 + (6-6)^2 + (8-6)^2 + (10-6)^2}{5} = \frac{16 + 4 + 0 + 4 + 16}{5} = 8$

3. Standard Deviation = $\sqrt{8} \approx 2.83$

Variance: Variance is the average of the squared differences from the mean. It is essentially the square of the standard deviation.

Formula: $\text{Variance} = \frac{\sum (x_i - \text{mean})^2}{n}$

---

2. Probability Distributions

Probability distributions describe how probabilities are distributed over the values of a random variable. Two common types are the normal distribution and the binomial distribution.

2.1 Normal Distribution

The normal distribution, also known as the Gaussian distribution, is a continuous probability distribution that is symmetric about the mean. It's characterized by its bell-shaped curve, where most values cluster around the mean.

Characteristics:

- **Mean** (μ): The center of the distribution.
- **Standard Deviation** (σ): Determines the spread of the distribution.
- **68-95-99.7 Rule**: Approximately 68% of data falls within one standard deviation of the mean, 95% within two standard deviations, and 99.7% within three standard deviations.

Example: Heights of adult men often follow a normal distribution. If the mean height is 70 inches with a standard deviation of 3 inches, then about 68% of men will have heights between 67 and 73 inches.

Visual Representation: The normal distribution is typically visualized as a bell curve, where the x-axis represents the values and the y-axis represents the probability density.

2.2 Binomial Distribution

The binomial distribution describes the number of successes in a fixed number of independent Bernoulli trials, each with the same probability of success.

Characteristics:

- **Number of Trials** (n): The total number of experiments or trials.
- **Probability of Success** (p): The probability of success in each trial.
- **Probability of Failure** (q): q=1−pq = 1 - pq=1−p
- **Number of Successes** (k): The number of successes in n trials.

Formula: P(X=k)=(nk)pk(1−p)n−kP(X = k) = \binom{n}{k} p^k (1 - p)^{n - k}P(X=k)=(kn)pk(1−p)n−k where (nk)\binom{n}{k}(kn) is the binomial coefficient representing the number of ways to choose k successes from n trials.

Example: If you flip a fair coin 10 times (n = 10) and want to find the probability of getting exactly 3 heads (k = 3) with a success probability (p) of 0.5:

P(X=3)=(103)(0.5)3(0.5)10−3P(X = 3) = \binom{10}{3} (0.5)^3 (0.5)^{10 - 3}P(X=3)=(310)(0.5)3(0.5)10−3 P(X=3)=10!3!(10−3)!(0.5)10P(X = 3) = \frac{10!}{3!(10 -

3)!} (0.5)^{10}P(X=3)=3!(10−3)!10!(0.5)10
P(X=3)=120×(0.5)10P(X = 3) = 120 \times (0.5)^{10}P(X=3)=120×(0.5)10 P(X=3)≈0.117P(X = 3) \approx 0.117P(X=3)≈0.117

Visual Representation: The binomial distribution is often visualized as a bar chart showing the probability of different numbers of successes.

Summary

Statistics and Probability are foundational to data science. The mean, median, and mode provide insights into the central tendency of data, while standard deviation and variance offer understanding of its spread. The normal distribution helps model continuous data, while the binomial distribution is used for discrete outcomes. Understanding these concepts enables better data analysis and informed decision-making in various domains.

This guide serves as a primer for these essential topics. Mastering these basics will pave the way for more advanced statistical methods and applications in data science.

Data Cleaning: Techniques for Handling Missing Data

and Outlier Detection

Introduction

Data cleaning is a crucial step in the data preprocessing pipeline. It involves identifying and correcting inaccuracies and inconsistencies in the data to ensure that it is accurate, complete, and usable for analysis. Two critical aspects of data cleaning are handling missing data and detecting and treating outliers. This guide provides a comprehensive overview of techniques for managing these issues, focusing on practical approaches that can be applied in various data science projects.

1. Handling Missing Data

Missing data can arise for numerous reasons, such as data entry errors, non-responses in surveys, or issues with data collection processes. It's essential to address missing data appropriately to ensure the integrity of your analysis.

1.1 Types of Missing Data

1. **Missing Completely at Random (MCAR):** The probability of missing data on a variable is independent of both observed and unobserved data.

For instance, if the data is missing randomly and not related to any specific pattern or characteristic, it is considered MCAR.

2. **Missing at Random (MAR)**: The probability of missing data on a variable is related to observed data but not the missing data itself. For example, if people with higher incomes are less likely to report their income, the missing data is related to income but not to the actual values of the missing data.

3. **Missing Not at Random (MNAR)**: The probability of missing data is related to the unobserved data. For example, if people with very high or very low income are less likely to report their income, the missing data is related to the income values themselves.

1.2 Techniques for Handling Missing Data

1. Deletion Methods

a. Listwise Deletion: This involves removing entire records with any missing values. While this method is straightforward, it can lead to a loss of valuable data and introduce bias if the missing data is not MCAR.

Example: Consider a dataset with the following rows:

ID	Age	Income
1	25	50000
2	NA	60000
3	30	NA
4	28	55000

Applying listwise deletion would remove rows 2 and 3, resulting in:

ID	Age	Income
1	25	50000
4	28	55000

b. Pairwise Deletion: This technique involves using all available data for each analysis, depending on which variables are present. It avoids deleting entire records but can be complex to manage and may introduce inconsistencies.

2. *Imputation Methods*

a. Mean/Median/Mode Imputation: Replace missing values with the mean (for continuous data), median (for skewed continuous data), or mode (for categorical data). This is simple but can reduce variability and may not always be appropriate.

Example: If the "Income" column is missing values, replacing missing values with the mean of the observed values:

ID	Age	Income
1	25	50000
2	28	55000
3	30	55000
4	28	55000

b. K-Nearest Neighbors (KNN) Imputation: Use the values from the nearest neighbors (similar records) to impute missing values. This method considers the similarity between records but can be computationally expensive.

c. Multiple Imputation: Create multiple datasets with imputed values, analyze each dataset separately, and then combine the results. This method provides a measure of uncertainty and is useful for handling missing data in more sophisticated ways.

d. Predictive Modeling: Use regression or other machine learning models to predict missing values based on other variables. For example, using a regression model where the missing value is the dependent variable and other variables are predictors.

Example: If income is missing, use age and other available features to predict the missing income values.

3. Data Augmentation

a. Using External Data: Augment your dataset with additional data sources that may contain the missing information. This approach is useful when external data can provide valuable insights or fill in gaps.

b. Data Simulation: Simulate the missing data based on known distributions or relationships in the data. This technique can be useful when dealing with missing data in a structured manner.

---

2. Outlier Detection and Treatment

Outliers are data points that significantly deviate from the rest of the data. They can arise from measurement errors, data entry mistakes, or natural variability in the data. Identifying and addressing outliers is crucial to ensure that they do not unduly influence your analysis.

2.1 Identifying Outliers

1. Statistical Methods

a. Z-Score: Calculate the Z-score for each data point, which measures how many standard deviations a point is from the mean. Outliers typically have Z-scores above a certain threshold (e.g., 3).

Formula: $Z = \frac{X - \text{mean}}{\text{standard deviation}}$

Example: For a dataset with a mean of 50 and a standard deviation of 10, a data point of 80 would have a Z-score of $\frac{80 - 50}{10} = 3$, indicating a potential outlier.

b. Interquartile Range (IQR): Identify outliers using the IQR, which measures the range between the first quartile (Q1) and the third quartile (Q3). Data points outside $Q1 - 1.5 \times \text{IQR}$ and $Q3 + 1.5 \times \text{IQR}$ are considered outliers.

Formula: $\text{IQR} = Q3 - Q1$

Example: For a dataset with Q1 = 25, Q3 = 75, and IQR = 50, data points outside the range $25 - 75$ and $75 + 75$ are outliers.

2. Graphical Methods

a. Box Plot: A box plot visually displays the distribution of data and highlights outliers. Data points that fall outside the whiskers of the box plot are considered outliers.

b. Scatter Plot: Use scatter plots to visualize data points and identify any that are significantly distant from the main cluster.

3. Model-Based Methods

a. Clustering: Use clustering algorithms (e.g., K-Means) to identify data points that do not fit well into any cluster, which may indicate outliers.

b. Statistical Tests: Apply statistical tests such as Grubbs' Test or Dixon's Q Test to formally assess the presence of outliers.

2.2 Treating Outliers

1. Removing Outliers

a. Simple Removal: Remove outliers from the dataset if they are clearly erroneous or if their presence skews the analysis. Ensure that this does not lead to significant loss of data or bias.

b. Threshold-Based Removal: Set thresholds based on statistical measures (e.g., Z-scores, IQR) and remove data points exceeding these thresholds.

2. Transforming Data

a. Log Transformation: Apply a logarithmic transformation to reduce the impact of extreme values. This can make the distribution more normal and less sensitive to outliers.

b. Winsorization: Cap extreme values at a specified percentile (e.g., 1st and 99th percentiles) to limit the effect of outliers while retaining data points.

Example: For a dataset with extreme values, replace values above the 95th percentile with the 95th percentile value.

3. Robust Methods

a. Robust Statistical Methods: Use statistical methods that are less sensitive to outliers, such as robust regression techniques that minimize the influence of extreme values.

b. Imputation: Replace outlier values with a more representative value (e.g., mean or median) based on the rest of the data.

4. **Validation and Sensitivity Analysis**

a. Re-evaluate Impact: After addressing outliers, re-evaluate the impact on your analysis. Ensure that the changes have improved the model performance and that important information has not been lost.

b. Sensitivity Analysis: Conduct sensitivity analysis to understand how outliers influence your results and whether removing or modifying them changes the conclusions.

Summary

Handling Missing Data involves choosing appropriate techniques based on the nature of the missingness, including deletion, imputation, and data augmentation. **Detecting and Treating Outliers** requires a combination of statistical, graphical, and model-based methods to identify and address data points that deviate significantly from the norm. By applying these techniques, you ensure that your data is clean, reliable, and ready for analysis, leading to more accurate and meaningful results.

This guide provides a foundational understanding of data cleaning techniques, equipping you with practical tools to address missing data and outliers effectively. Mastering these concepts will enhance your ability to preprocess data and prepare it for further analysis, contributing to more robust and insightful findings in your data science projects.

Introduction to Machine Learning: Supervised vs. Unsupervised Learning, Overfitting vs. Underfitting

Introduction

Machine learning (ML) is a transformative field within artificial intelligence (AI) that empowers systems to learn from data and improve their performance over time without being explicitly programmed. The core of machine learning revolves around various techniques and algorithms that can be broadly classified into supervised and unsupervised learning. Additionally, understanding concepts such as overfitting and underfitting is crucial for building effective models. This guide offers an in-depth introduction to these foundational concepts in machine learning.

1. Supervised Learning

Supervised learning is a type of machine learning where the model is trained on labeled data. The goal is to learn a mapping from inputs (features) to outputs (labels) such that the model can make accurate predictions on new, unseen data.

1.1 Definition

Supervised Learning involves training a model on a dataset that includes both input features and corresponding output labels. The model learns from this data to predict the output labels for new, unseen inputs. The process is guided by the supervision provided by the labeled data, hence the name "supervised."

Examples:

- **Classification**: Predicting discrete labels. For instance, classifying emails as "spam" or "not spam."
- **Regression**: Predicting continuous values. For example, forecasting house prices based on features like size, location, and number of rooms.

1.2 Common Algorithms

1. **Linear Regression**: Used for regression tasks. It models the relationship between input features and

a continuous output by fitting a linear equation to the data.

Formula: $y = \beta_0 + \beta_1 x_1 + \beta_2 x_2 + \cdots + \beta_n x_n$ where y is the predicted value, β_0 is the intercept, and $\beta_1, \beta_2, \ldots, \beta_n$ are coefficients for the input features $x_1, x_2, \ldots, x_n$.

2. **Logistic Regression**: A classification algorithm that predicts the probability of a binary outcome. It uses a logistic function to model the relationship between input features and the probability of the target class.

Formula: $p = \dfrac{1}{1 + e^{-(\beta_0 + \beta_1 x_1 + \beta_2 x_2 + \cdots + \beta_n x_n)}}$ where p is the probability of the positive class.

3. **Decision Trees**: These algorithms split the data into subsets based on feature values, creating a tree-like structure where each internal node represents a feature test and each leaf node represents an output label.

4. **Support Vector Machines (SVM)**: A classification algorithm that finds the hyperplane that best separates different classes in the feature space. It can handle both linear and non-linear classification problems.

5. **Neural Networks**: Models inspired by biological neural networks, consisting of layers of interconnected nodes (neurons). They can learn complex patterns through training.

2. Unsupervised Learning

Unsupervised learning involves training a model on data without labeled responses. The goal is to identify patterns, structures, or relationships within the data.

2.1 Definition

Unsupervised Learning deals with finding hidden structures or intrinsic patterns in input data. Unlike supervised learning, there are no explicit labels or targets for the model to learn from. The model seeks to discover the underlying structure or distribution of the data.

Examples:

- **Clustering**: Grouping similar data points together. For example, customer segmentation in marketing based on purchasing behavior.

- **Dimensionality Reduction**: Reducing the number of features while retaining essential information. For instance, principal component analysis (PCA) is used to visualize high-dimensional data in 2D or 3D.

2.2 Common Algorithms

1. **K-Means Clustering**: A partitioning method that divides the data into kkk clusters by minimizing the variance within each cluster.

Algorithm:

1. Initialize kkk cluster centroids.
2. Assign each data point to the nearest centroid.

> 3. Update centroids based on the mean of the assigned data points.
> 4. Repeat steps 2 and 3 until convergence.

2. **Hierarchical Clustering**: Builds a hierarchy of clusters through either agglomerative (bottom-up) or divisive (top-down) approaches. It produces a dendrogram that shows the nested grouping of data points.

3. **Principal Component Analysis (PCA)**: A dimensionality reduction technique that transforms data into a set of orthogonal components, ordered by the amount of variance they capture.

4. **t-Distributed Stochastic Neighbor Embedding (t-SNE)**: A non-linear dimensionality reduction technique primarily used for visualization. It preserves local structures in the data.

5. **Association Rules**: Identifies relationships or associations between variables in large datasets. For instance, market basket analysis to find items frequently bought together.

---

3. Overfitting vs. Underfitting

In machine learning, overfitting and underfitting are issues that impact model performance. Understanding these concepts is essential for building models that generalize well to new data.

3.1 Overfitting

Overfitting occurs when a model learns the details and noise in the training data to the extent that it performs poorly on new, unseen data. The model is too complex and captures patterns that do not generalize beyond the training set.

Characteristics:

- High accuracy on training data.
- Poor accuracy on validation or test data.
- The model has high variance and low bias.

Causes:

- **Too Complex Model:** Using a model with too many parameters or high capacity (e.g., deep neural networks) can lead to overfitting.
- **Insufficient Data:** Training on a small dataset can cause the model to learn noise and outliers.

Detection:

- **Validation Curves:** Plotting training and validation error can show overfitting if the training error continues to decrease while validation error increases.
- **Cross-Validation:** Evaluating the model's performance on multiple validation sets can reveal overfitting.

Prevention:

- **Regularization:** Techniques like L1 (Lasso) and L2 (Ridge) regularization add penalties to large coefficients, encouraging simpler models.

- **Pruning:** In decision trees, pruning removes branches that have little importance, reducing complexity.
- **Early Stopping:** Halting the training process before the model begins to overfit the data.
- **Data Augmentation:** Increasing the amount of training data through augmentation techniques can help generalize better.

3.2 Underfitting

Underfitting occurs when a model is too simple to capture the underlying patterns in the data. It results in poor performance on both training and test datasets because the model has high bias and low variance.

Characteristics:

- Poor accuracy on both training and validation data.
- The model fails to capture important patterns or relationships in the data.

Causes:

- **Too Simple Model:** Using a model with insufficient complexity (e.g., linear regression for a non-linear problem).
- **Insufficient Features:** Missing important features or using overly simplified features.

Detection:

- **High Bias:** Consistently high training error indicates that the model is too simple.

- **Learning Curves**: Plots of training and validation error that converge to a high error value suggest underfitting.

Prevention:

- **Increasing Model Complexity**: Using more complex models or adding more features can help capture the underlying patterns.
- **Feature Engineering**: Creating new features or transforming existing ones to better represent the data.
- **Polynomial Features**: Adding polynomial features to capture non-linear relationships in the data.

Summary

Understanding **supervised and unsupervised learning** is fundamental to machine learning. Supervised learning leverages labeled data to train models that can predict outcomes, while unsupervised learning explores unlabeled data to discover patterns and structures. **Overfitting** and **underfitting** are key concepts in model evaluation and improvement. Overfitting occurs when a model learns noise and performs poorly on new data, while underfitting happens when a model is too simple to capture the underlying data patterns. Effective machine learning requires balancing model complexity and ensuring that the model generalizes well to new data.

This guide provides a solid foundation in these core concepts, equipping you with the knowledge needed to navigate the challenges of building and evaluating machine learning models. Mastering these principles will enhance your ability to create models that deliver accurate and reliable predictions.

Intermediate Machine Learning Algorithms: Decision Trees and k-Nearest Neighbors (k-NN)

Introduction

In machine learning, selecting the right algorithm is crucial for building effective models. Two widely used algorithms are **Decision Trees** and **k-Nearest Neighbors (k-NN)**. Each has its own strengths and is suited to different types of problems. This guide delves into these algorithms, providing a detailed explanation of how they work, their advantages, and their applications.

1. Decision Trees

Decision Trees are a popular and versatile machine learning algorithm used for both classification and regression tasks. They model decisions and their possible consequences as a tree structure, which makes them easy to interpret and visualize.

1.1 Definition and Structure

A decision tree is a flowchart-like structure where:

- **Internal Nodes** represent tests on features (e.g., whether a feature value is less than a certain threshold).
- **Branches** represent the outcome of the test and connect nodes.
- **Leaf Nodes** represent the final decision or output (e.g., class labels or continuous values).

The tree starts at a **root node** and splits into branches based on feature tests. This process continues recursively, creating **sub-trees** until it reaches **leaf nodes** that provide the final prediction.

1.2 How Decision Trees Work

1.2.1 Building the Tree

The construction of a decision tree involves selecting the best feature to split the data at each node. The goal is to choose splits that maximize the separation of classes or minimize prediction errors. The process generally involves:

1. **Selecting a Feature to Split On:** Choose the feature that provides the best split according to a criterion (e.g., Gini impurity, Information Gain, or Mean Squared Error).

Criteria for Split:

- **Gini Impurity:** Measures how often a randomly chosen element from the set would be incorrectly labeled if it was randomly labeled according to the distribution of labels in the set.

Formula: $Gini = 1 - \sum_{i=1}^{C}(p_i)^2$ where p_i is the probability of an element being classified into class i and C is the number of classes.

- **Information Gain:** Measures the reduction in entropy or impurity after a split. Entropy is the measure of unpredictability or the amount of disorder in the dataset.

Formula:
$$IG = Entropy(Parent) - \sum_{i=1}^{n} \frac{|Subset_i|}{|Parent|} \cdot Entropy(Subset_i)$$

- **Mean Squared Error (MSE):** Used for regression trees. Measures the average squared difference between actual and predicted values.

Formula: $MSE = \frac{1}{N} \sum_{i=1}^{N} (y_i - \hat{y}_i)^2$ where y_i is the actual value, $\hat{y}_i$ is the predicted value, and N is the number of samples.

2. **Splitting the Data:** Based on the selected feature and split criterion, divide the dataset into subsets.
3. **Recursively Repeating:** Repeat the process for each subset, creating sub-trees until:
    - A stopping criterion is met (e.g., a maximum depth of the tree, minimum number of samples per leaf, or no further improvement in split quality).
    - All data points in a node belong to the same class or have very similar values (in regression).

1.2.2 Example

Consider a simple example where we want to classify whether a person will buy a product based on their age and income:

- **Age:** Young, Middle-aged, Senior
- **Income:** Low, Medium, High

The decision tree might look like this:

1. **Root Node:** Split on **Income**.
    - **Low:** Classify as **No Buy**.
    - **Medium/High:** Further split on **Age**.
        - **Young:** Classify as **No Buy**.
        - **Middle-aged/Senior:** Classify as **Buy**.

1.3 Advantages and Disadvantages

Advantages:

- **Easy to Interpret:** The tree structure makes it easy to understand how decisions are made.
- **No Feature Scaling Required:** Decision trees do not require normalization or standardization of features.
- **Handles Both Categorical and Numerical Data:** Can work with various types of data.

Disadvantages:

- **Overfitting:** Decision trees can easily overfit the training data, especially if they grow too deep.
- **Instability:** Small changes in the data can result in a completely different tree structure.
- **Bias:** Decision trees can be biased towards features with more levels.

Mitigation Strategies:

- **Pruning:** Reducing the size of the tree by removing branches that have little importance.
- **Ensemble Methods:** Combining multiple trees (e.g., Random Forests, Gradient Boosting) to improve performance and stability.

---

2. k-Nearest Neighbors (k-NN)

k-Nearest Neighbors (k-NN) is a simple and intuitive machine learning algorithm used for classification and regression. It operates on the principle of finding the most similar data points in the feature space to make predictions.

2.1 Definition and Working Principle

k-NN is a lazy learning algorithm that does not build a model but makes decisions based on the proximity of data points. It predicts the class or value of a data point by looking at its k-nearest neighbors in the feature space.

1. Choosing k: The number of neighbors (k) to consider. The choice of k affects the algorithm's performance.

2. **Distance Metric:** Measures the similarity between data points. Common metrics include:

    - **Euclidean Distance:** The straight-line distance between two points.

Formula: $d(x,y) = \sqrt{\sum_{i=1}^{n} (x_i - y_i)^2}$

    - **Manhattan Distance:** The sum of absolute differences between coordinates.

Formula: $d(x, y) = \sum_{i=1}^{n} |x_i - y_i|$

    - **Minkowski Distance:** A generalized distance metric that includes Euclidean and Manhattan distances as special cases.

Formula: $d(x, y) = \left(\sum_{i=1}^{n} |x_i - y_i|^p \right)^{\frac{1}{p}}$

3. **Predicting:**

- **Classification**: Assign the class that is most frequent among the k-nearest neighbors.
- **Regression**: Compute the average of the values of the k-nearest neighbors.

Example:

Suppose we want to classify whether a new email is spam or not based on features such as word count, frequency of certain keywords, etc. For a new email, the k-NN algorithm will:

1. Calculate the distance between this email and all other emails in the training set.
2. Identify the k-nearest emails (e.g., k=5).
3. Determine the class based on the majority class of these nearest neighbors.

2.2 Advantages and Disadvantages

Advantages:

- **Simple and Easy to Understand**: Intuitive and straightforward to implement.
- **No Training Phase**: Does not require a training phase as it makes predictions directly from the data.
- **Adaptable**: Can be used for both classification and regression tasks.

Disadvantages:

- **Computationally Intensive**: Requires distance computation for each query point, which can be slow for large datasets.

- **Sensitive to Irrelevant Features**: The presence of irrelevant features can affect the performance of k-NN.
- **Choice of k**: The performance of the algorithm depends on the choice of k and distance metric. An inappropriate k can lead to poor results.

Mitigation Strategies:

- **Feature Scaling**: Normalize or standardize features to ensure that no single feature dominates the distance metric.
- **Dimensionality Reduction**: Use techniques like PCA to reduce the number of features and improve performance.
- **Efficient Data Structures**: Implement algorithms like KD-Trees or Ball Trees to speed up the nearest neighbor search.

Summary

Decision Trees and **k-Nearest Neighbors (k-NN)** are fundamental machine learning algorithms with distinct characteristics and applications. **Decision Trees** offer a clear, interpretable model structure for both classification and regression tasks, but can suffer from overfitting and instability. **k-NN**, on the other hand, is a simple, instance-based learning algorithm that relies on the proximity of data points to make predictions, but can be computationally intensive and sensitive to feature scaling.

Understanding these algorithms' mechanics, advantages, and limitations is crucial for selecting the right approach for a given problem and optimizing model performance. This guide provides a solid foundation in these intermediate machine learning algorithms, enhancing your ability to implement and fine-tune them for various applications.

Model Evaluation: Cross-Validation Techniques, Precision, Recall, and F1-Score

Introduction

Evaluating the performance of machine learning models is crucial for ensuring they generalize well to unseen data. Effective evaluation helps in understanding how well a model performs and where it might need improvement. This guide delves into two key aspects of model evaluation: **cross-validation techniques** and the metrics **precision, recall,** and **F1-score**. These methods and metrics provide a comprehensive approach to assessing the quality and reliability of machine learning models.

---

1. Cross-Validation Techniques

Cross-validation is a statistical technique used to estimate the performance of a machine learning model on unseen data. It helps to assess how the model generalizes to an independent dataset, reducing the risk of overfitting. Here, we explore several cross-validation methods and their applications.

1.1 Definition and Purpose

Cross-validation involves partitioning a dataset into multiple subsets or folds to evaluate a model's performance. The model is trained on some folds and tested on the remaining folds, iterating through different partitions to ensure robust performance evaluation.

1.2 Types of Cross-Validation

1.2.1 K-Fold Cross-Validation

In **k-Fold Cross-Validation**, the dataset is divided into kkk equal-sized folds. The model is trained on $k-1k-$

$k-1$ folds and tested on the remaining fold. This process is repeated k times, each time with a different fold as the test set. The performance metrics are averaged over all k iterations to provide a final evaluation.

Steps:

1. **Split Data:** Divide the dataset into k folds.
2. **Train and Test:** For each fold, train the model on $k-1$ folds and test it on the remaining fold.
3. **Aggregate Results:** Compute performance metrics for each iteration and average them.

Advantages:

- Provides a more accurate estimate of model performance compared to a single train-test split.
- Uses all data for both training and testing, which maximizes the utility of the dataset.

Disadvantages:

- Computationally expensive, especially with large datasets and high k.
- May still suffer from variability if k is not chosen appropriately.

Example: For $k=5$, the dataset is divided into 5 folds. The model is trained and evaluated 5 times, each time using a different fold as the test set and the remaining 4 folds as the training set. The average performance across all 5 iterations is used to assess the model's effectiveness.

1.2.2 Leave-One-Out Cross-Validation (LOOCV)

Leave-One-Out Cross-Validation is a special case of k-Fold Cross-Validation where k equals the number of data points. Each data point is used as a test set once, with all other points as the training set.

Advantages:

- Provides an almost unbiased estimate of model performance.
- Useful for small datasets where each data point is valuable.

Disadvantages:

- Computationally intensive, as the model is trained N times, where N is the number of data points.
- May not be practical for large datasets.

Example: In a dataset with 100 data points, LOOCV involves training the model 100 times, each time leaving out one data point for testing.

1.2.3 Stratified K-Fold Cross-Validation

Stratified K-Fold Cross-Validation is an extension of k-Fold Cross-Validation that ensures each fold maintains the proportion of classes found in the entire dataset. It is particularly useful for imbalanced datasets where some classes are underrepresented.

Advantages:

- Ensures that each fold is representative of the overall class distribution.
- Provides a more reliable estimate of model performance for classification tasks.

Disadvantages:

- Slightly more complex to implement compared to standard k-Fold Cross-Validation.
- Computationally intensive if kkk is large.

Example: In a dataset with 80% positive and 20% negative examples, each fold in Stratified k-Fold will also have approximately 80% positive and 20% negative examples, ensuring balanced representation.

1.2.4 Time Series Cross-Validation

Time Series Cross-Validation is used for time-dependent data where observations are sequential. It involves creating training and test sets in a way that respects the temporal order of data.

Steps:

1. **Initial Split:** Train on initial data points and test on subsequent points.
2. **Rolling Window:** Expand the training set progressively while moving the test set forward in time.

Advantages:

- Maintains the temporal order of data, which is crucial for time series forecasting.

Disadvantages:

- May lead to less data being used for training as the test set moves forward.
- Requires careful consideration of how to split data while respecting time dependencies.

Example: In a time series dataset, you might train the model on data from January to June and test it on July, then expand the training set to include July and test on August, and so on.

---

2. Precision, Recall, and F1-Score

Precision, Recall, and **F1-Score** are metrics used to evaluate the performance of classification models, especially in scenarios with imbalanced classes. These metrics provide insights into different aspects of model performance.

2.1 Definition and Importance

- **Precision** measures the proportion of true positive predictions among all positive predictions made by the model. It indicates how many of the predicted positives are actually positive.

Formula: $\text{Precision} = \frac{TP}{TP + FP}$ where TP is the number of true positives, and FP is the number of false positives.

- **Recall** (or Sensitivity) measures the proportion of true positive predictions among all actual positive instances. It indicates how many of the actual positives were correctly identified by the model.

Formula: $\text{Recall} = \frac{TP}{TP + FN}$ where TP is the number of true positives, and FN is the number of false negatives.

- **F1-Score** is the harmonic mean of Precision and Recall. It provides a single metric that balances both precision and recall, making it useful when dealing with imbalanced datasets.

Formula:

$$\text{F1-Score} = 2 \times \frac{\text{Precision} \times \text{Recall}}{\text{Precision} + \text{Recall}}$$

2.2 Examples and Interpretations

Example 1: Consider a medical test for a rare disease. Out of 1000 patients:

- 50 have the disease (positive cases), and 950 do not (negative cases).
- The model predicts 40 positive cases correctly and 10 false positives.

Precision:

$$\text{Precision} = \frac{40}{40 + 10} = \frac{40}{50} = 0.80$$

Recall:

$$\text{Recall} = \frac{40}{40 + 10} = \frac{40}{50} = 0.80$$

F1-Score:

$$\text{F1-Score} = 2 \times \frac{0.80 \times 0.80}{0.80 + 0.80} = 0.80$$

Example 2: In a fraud detection system:

- 100 transactions are fraudulent (positive), and 900 are not (negative).
- The model identifies 70 fraudulent transactions correctly but misses 30 (false negatives) and incorrectly flags 20 legitimate transactions as fraudulent.

Precision: $\text{Precision} = \frac{70}{70 + 20} = \frac{70}{90} = 0.78$

Recall: $\text{Recall} = \frac{70}{70 + 30} = \frac{70}{100} = 0.70$

F1-Score: $\text{F1-Score} = 2 \times \frac{0.78 \times 0.70}{0.78 + 0.70} = 0.74$

2.3 Choosing the Right Metric

- **Precision** is critical when the cost of false positives is high. For example, in spam detection, marking a legitimate email as spam (false positive) may be more problematic than missing some spam emails (false negatives).

- **Recall** is crucial when missing positive instances has significant consequences. For example, in disease screening, failing to identify a patient with the disease (false negative) is more serious than a false alarm (false positive).

- **F1-Score** is useful when you need a balanced view of precision and recall, especially in imbalanced datasets where neither precision nor recall alone provides a complete picture.

Summary

Effective model evaluation involves understanding and applying cross-validation techniques and performance metrics. **Cross-validation** techniques, such as k-Fold, LOOCV, Stratified k-Fold, and Time Series Cross-

Validation, offer various methods to assess model performance and reduce overfitting risks. **Precision, Recall,** and **F1-Score** provide insights into classification performance, particularly in imbalanced datasets.

By leveraging these techniques and metrics, you can better understand your model's capabilities, make informed decisions about its deployment, and continuously improve its performance. This comprehensive approach to model evaluation ensures that your machine learning models are both robust and reliable.

Feature Engineering: Feature Scaling, Normalization, and Dimensionality Reduction

Introduction

Feature engineering is a critical step in the machine learning pipeline that significantly impacts the performance of a model. Two fundamental aspects of feature engineering are **feature scaling and normalization** and **dimensionality reduction**. These techniques prepare and transform data to enhance the effectiveness of machine learning algorithms. This guide explores these concepts in detail, focusing on their importance, methods, and practical applications.

1. Feature Scaling and Normalization

Feature scaling and normalization are techniques used to adjust the range and distribution of feature values in a dataset. These processes ensure that features contribute equally to the model, particularly in algorithms sensitive to feature scales.

1.1 Feature Scaling

Feature Scaling is the process of adjusting the range of feature values. This is essential because many machine learning algorithms, especially those relying on distance metrics, are sensitive to the scale of input features.

Common Scaling Methods:

1.1.1 Min-Max Scaling

Min-Max Scaling (or normalization) transforms features to a fixed range, typically [0, 1]. This technique is useful when you want to maintain the relative relationships between feature values.

Formula: $X_{\text{scaled}} = \frac{X - X_{\text{min}}}{X_{\text{max}} - X_{\text{min}}}$

- X: Original feature value
- X_{min}: Minimum value of the feature
- X_{max}: Maximum value of the feature

- **X_scaled**: Scaled feature value

Example: Suppose a feature "age" has a minimum value of 20 and a maximum value of 70. An age value of 40 would be scaled as:

$$X_{\text{scaled}} = \frac{40 - 20}{70 - 20} = \frac{20}{50} = 0.40$$

1.1.2 Standardization (Z-Score Normalization)

Standardization (or Z-Score Normalization) transforms features to have a mean of 0 and a standard deviation of 1. This method is useful for algorithms that assume normally distributed data.

Formula: $X_{\text{standardized}} = \frac{X - \mu}{\sigma}$

- **X**: Original feature value
- **μ**: Mean of the feature
- **σ**: Standard deviation of the feature
- **X_standardized**: Standardized feature value

Example: If the "age" feature has a mean of 45 and a standard deviation of 10, an age value of 40 would be standardized as:

$$X_{\text{standardized}} = \frac{40 - 45}{10} = -0.50$$

1.1.3 Robust Scaling

Robust Scaling uses the median and the interquartile range (IQR) to scale features, making it less sensitive to outliers.

Formula: $X_{\text{robust}} = \frac{X - \text{median}}{\text{IQR}}$

- **X**: Original feature value
- **Median**: Median of the feature
- **IQR**: Interquartile range (75th percentile - 25th percentile)
- **X_robust**: Robustly scaled feature value

Example: If the "age" feature has a median of 45 and an IQR of 20, an age value of 40 would be scaled as: $X_{\text{robust}} = \frac{40 - 45}{20} = -0.25$

Advantages of Feature Scaling:

- **Improves Convergence**: Scaling can speed up the convergence of gradient-based algorithms.
- **Equal Contribution**: Ensures all features contribute equally to the model, especially in distance-based algorithms.
- **Avoids Bias**: Prevents features with larger scales from dominating the model.

Disadvantages:

- **Sensitivity to Outliers**: Some scaling methods are sensitive to outliers and may not be robust.

1.2 Feature Normalization

Feature Normalization refers to adjusting the scale of features to fit within a certain range. Normalization ensures that all features contribute equally to model training.

Common Normalization Methods:

1.2.1 L1 Normalization (Manhattan Norm)

L1 Normalization scales features so that the sum of the absolute values equals 1.

Formula: $X_{\text{normalized}} = \frac{X}{\sum_{i=1}^{n} |X_i|}$

- X: Original feature value
- $\Sigma |X_i|$: Sum of the absolute values of the feature
- $X_{normalized}$: Normalized feature value

Example: If a feature vector is [2, 3, 4], the L1 normalization would be:
$$X_{\text{normalized}} = \frac{[2, 3, 4]}{2 + 3 + 4} = \frac{[2, 3, 4]}{9} = [0.22, 0.33, 0.44]$$

1.2.2 L2 Normalization (Euclidean Norm)

L2 Normalization scales features so that the sum of the squared values equals 1.

Formula: $X_{\text{normalized}} = \frac{X}{\sqrt{\sum_{i=1}^{n} X_i^2}}$

- X: Original feature value
- $\sqrt{\Sigma(X_i^2)}$: Square root of the sum of squared feature values
- $X_{normalized}$: Normalized feature value

Example: If a feature vector is [2, 3, 4], the L2 normalization would be:
$X_{\text{normalized}} = \frac{[2,3,4]}{\sqrt{2^2+3^2+4^2}} = \frac{[2,3,4]}{5.38} = [0.37, 0.56, 0.$

$$X_{\text{normalized}} = \frac{[2, 3, 4]}{\sqrt{2^2 + 3^2 + 4^2}} = \frac{[2, 3, 4]}{5.38} = [0.37, 0.56, 0.74]$$

Advantages of Normalization:

- **Improves Performance**: Essential for algorithms that rely on distance metrics.
- **Equal Weighting**: Ensures all features have a comparable scale, preventing bias in model training.

Disadvantages:

- **Data Dependency**: Requires that features have similar distributions or ranges.

---

2. Dimensionality Reduction

Dimensionality Reduction techniques reduce the number of features in a dataset while retaining as much information as possible. These techniques are valuable for improving model performance, reducing computational cost, and mitigating the curse of dimensionality.

2.1 Principal Component Analysis (PCA)

Principal Component Analysis (PCA) is a widely used dimensionality reduction technique that transforms data into a new coordinate system. It identifies the principal components (directions of maximum variance) and projects data onto these components.

Steps in PCA:

2.1.1 Standardization

Standardize the features to have zero mean and unit variance, especially if features are on different scales.

2.1.2 Covariance Matrix Computation

Calculate the covariance matrix of the standardized features to understand the variance and correlation between features.

Formula:
$$\text{Cov}(X, Y) = \frac{1}{n-1} \sum_{i=1}^{n} (X_i - \bar{X})(Y_i - \bar{Y})$$

- X and Y: Features
- n: Number of data points
- Cov(X, Y): Covariance between X and Y

2.1.3 Eigenvalue and Eigenvector Computation

Compute the eigenvalues and eigenvectors of the covariance matrix. Eigenvectors represent the directions of maximum variance (principal components), and eigenvalues represent the magnitude of variance along these directions.

2.1.4 Projection

Project the data onto the top k principal components (eigenvectors with the largest eigenvalues) to reduce dimensionality.

Formula: $X_{\text{reduced}} = X \cdot W$

- X: Original data matrix
- W: Matrix of selected eigenvectors

- **X_reduced**: Reduced data matrix

Example: Given a dataset with features X_1 and X_2, PCA might transform the data to new features Z_1 and Z_2 where Z_1 captures the most variance, and Z_2 captures the remaining variance.

Advantages of PCA:

- **Reduces Complexity**: Simplifies models by reducing the number of features.
- **Improves Performance**: Can lead to better model performance by removing noisy or irrelevant features.
- **Visualization**: Enables visualization of high-dimensional data in 2D or 3D.

Disadvantages:

- **Loss of Interpretability**: Transformed features (principal components) may be less interpretable.
- **Assumption of Linearity**: PCA assumes linear relationships between features, which may not always be applicable.

2.2 Other Dimensionality Reduction Techniques

2.2.1 Linear Discriminant Analysis (LDA)

Linear Discriminant Analysis (LDA) is a supervised dimensionality reduction technique that maximizes the separation between classes while reducing dimensionality. Unlike PCA, which is unsupervised, LDA takes class labels into account.

Steps:

1. Compute the within-class and between-class scatter matrices.
2. Compute the eigenvalues and eigenvectors of the matrix derived from these scatter matrices.
3. Project data onto the eigenvectors corresponding to the largest eigenvalues.

Advantages:

- **Class Separation:** Enhances class separation by considering class labels.
- **Improves Classification:** Often leads to better performance in classification tasks.

Disadvantages:

- **Requires Class Labels:** Not applicable for unsupervised learning tasks.
- **Assumes Normality:** Assumes that features are normally distributed within each class.

2.2.2 t-Distributed Stochastic Neighbor Embedding (t-SNE)

t-Distributed Stochastic Neighbor Embedding (t-SNE) is a technique designed for visualizing high-dimensional data in 2D or 3D space. It focuses on preserving the local structure of data.

Steps:

1. Compute pairwise similarities between data points in high-dimensional space.
2. Compute pairwise similarities in the lower-dimensional space.

3. Minimize the divergence between these similarities using optimization techniques.

Advantages:

- **Effective Visualization**: Excellent for visualizing clusters and patterns in high-dimensional data.
- **Non-Linear**: Captures non-linear relationships in the data.

Disadvantages:

- **Computationally Intensive**: Can be slow for large datasets.
- **Not Suitable for Classification**: Primarily a visualization tool, not intended for classification tasks.

Summary

Feature scaling and normalization ensure that features are on comparable scales, which is essential for algorithms sensitive to feature magnitudes and distances. **Dimensionality reduction** techniques, such as PCA, help in simplifying models and improving performance by reducing the number of features while retaining critical information.

- **Feature Scaling** (Min-Max Scaling, Standardization, Robust Scaling) adjusts feature values to a common scale.
- **Feature Normalization** (L1 and L2 Normalization) adjusts features to fit within a specific range or norm.

- ***Dimensionality Reduction*** *(PCA, LDA, t-SNE) reduces the number of features while preserving essential information.*

By understanding and applying these techniques, you can enhance your machine learning models' performance, interpretability, and efficiency, leading to more robust and reliable data-driven solutions.

Advanced Data Science Concepts: Deep Learning

Introduction

Deep learning is a subset of machine learning that involves neural networks with multiple layers, known as deep neural networks. This approach has revolutionized fields such as computer vision, natural language processing, and speech recognition. In this guide, we will explore the architecture of neural networks and delve into convolutional neural networks (CNNs) and their applications.

---

1. Architecture of Neural Networks

Neural Networks are computational models inspired by the human brain's structure and function. They consist of interconnected layers of nodes, called neurons, which process data by learning patterns and features from input data.

1.1 Basic Components

1.1.1 Neurons

Neurons are the fundamental units of a neural network. Each neuron receives input from multiple sources, processes the input using an activation function, and passes the result to the next layer.

Key Functions:

- **Weights**: Adjust the importance of inputs.
- **Biases**: Provide additional flexibility by shifting the activation function.
- **Activation Function**: Determines if a neuron should be activated based on its input.

1.1.2 Activation Functions

Activation functions introduce non-linearity into the model, allowing it to learn complex patterns. Common activation functions include:

- **Sigmoid Function**: $\sigma(x) = \frac{1}{1 + e^{-x}}$
    - **Range**: (0, 1)
    - **Usage**: Common in binary classification problems.

- **ReLU (Rectified Linear Unit)**: $\text{ReLU}(x) = \max(0, x)$
    - **Range**: $[0, \infty)$
    - **Usage**: Widely used in hidden layers of deep neural networks due to its efficiency and simplicity.

- **Tanh (Hyperbolic Tangent)**: $\tanh(x) = \frac{e^x - e^{-x}}{e^x + e^{-x}}$
    - **Range**: (-1, 1)
    - **Usage**: Used in situations where data normalization is needed.

1.1.3 Layers

Neural networks are composed of several types of layers, each serving a specific purpose:

- **Input Layer**: Receives the raw data and passes it to the subsequent layers.
- **Hidden Layers**: Perform computations and feature extraction. These can be fully connected (dense)

layers or specialized layers, depending on the network type.

- **Output Layer**: Produces the final output of the network. The choice of activation function in the output layer depends on the type of problem (e.g., softmax for multi-class classification).

1.1.4 Training Process

Training a neural network involves adjusting weights and biases using a dataset and an optimization algorithm. The primary steps are:

1. **Forward Propagation**: Data is passed through the network to generate predictions.

2. **Loss Calculation**: The difference between predictions and actual values is computed using a loss function (e.g., mean squared error for regression, cross-entropy loss for classification).

3. **Backpropagation**: Gradients of the loss function with respect to the weights are calculated using the chain rule.

4. **Optimization**: Weights are updated using optimization algorithms such as Gradient Descent or Adam to minimize the loss.

1.1.5 Optimization Algorithms

- **Gradient Descent**: Iteratively updates weights by moving in the direction of the negative gradient of the loss function.

- **Adam (Adaptive Moment Estimation)**: Combines the benefits of both AdaGrad and RMSProp, adjusting learning rates based on the first and second moments of the gradients.

1.1.6 Regularization Techniques

Regularization techniques prevent overfitting and improve generalization:

- **L1 and L2 Regularization**: Add a penalty term to the loss function based on the magnitude of the weights.
- **Dropout**: Randomly drops neurons during training to prevent dependency on specific neurons and improve generalization.
- **Batch Normalization**: Normalizes the input of each layer to stabilize learning and improve convergence.

---

2. Convolutional Neural Networks (CNNs)

Convolutional Neural Networks (CNNs) are a specialized type of neural network designed for processing grid-like data, such as images. They excel at extracting spatial hierarchies and patterns, making them highly effective for tasks in computer vision.

2.1 Architecture of CNNs

2.1.1 Convolutional Layers

Convolutional layers apply convolution operations to the input data, using filters (kernels) to detect features such as edges, textures, and shapes.

Key Components:

- **Filters (Kernels)**: Small matrices that slide over the input data to produce feature maps. Each filter detects specific features.
- **Stride**: The step size with which the filter moves across the input data. Larger strides result in smaller feature maps.
- **Padding**: Adding extra pixels around the input data to control the size of the output feature maps and preserve spatial dimensions.

Formula: $\text{Output} = (X - F + 2P) / S + 1$

- **X**: Size of the input
- **F**: Size of the filter
- **P**: Padding
- **S**: Stride
- **Output**: Size of the output feature map

Example: If you apply a 3×3 filter with a stride of 1 to a 32×32 image with no padding, the resulting feature map will be 30×30.

2.1.2 Pooling Layers

Pooling layers reduce the spatial dimensions of feature maps, making the network less sensitive to small translations and reducing computational complexity.

Common Pooling Methods:

- **Max Pooling**: Selects the maximum value from a pool of values.

- **Average Pooling**: Computes the average value from a pool of values.

Formula: For a 2×2 max pooling operation: $\text{Output} = \text{max}(X_1, X_2, X_3, X_4)$ where X_i are the values in the pooling region.

2.1.3 Fully Connected Layers

Fully connected (dense) layers follow convolutional and pooling layers. They combine features extracted by previous layers to make final predictions. Each neuron in a fully connected layer is connected to every neuron in the previous layer.

2.1.4 Activation Functions

ReLU is commonly used in CNNs to introduce non-linearity and improve training efficiency. Other activation functions like sigmoid or tanh can also be used, depending on the specific application.

2.1.5 Example Architecture

A typical CNN architecture might include:

1. **Input Layer**: Takes raw image data.
2. **Convolutional Layer**: Applies several filters to detect features.
3. **Activation Layer (ReLU)**: Introduces non-linearity.
4. **Pooling Layer**: Reduces spatial dimensions.
5. **Convolutional Layer**: Applies additional filters.
6. **Activation Layer (ReLU)**: Introduces non-linearity.
7. **Pooling Layer**: Further reduces dimensions.

8. **Fully Connected Layer**: Combines features for classification or regression.
9. **Output Layer**: Produces final predictions (e.g., class probabilities).

---

3. Applications of CNNs

CNNs have been widely adopted in various domains due to their ability to effectively capture spatial hierarchies and patterns. Here are some prominent applications:

3.1 Image Classification

CNNs are extensively used for classifying images into categories. They can recognize objects, animals, or scenes based on learned features.

Example: The ImageNet competition, which involves classifying thousands of categories, has seen significant success with CNN-based models such as AlexNet, VGGNet, and ResNet.

3.2 Object Detection

Object detection involves identifying and locating objects within an image. CNNs are used to detect multiple objects, draw bounding boxes, and classify each object.

Example: Models like YOLO (You Only Look Once) and SSD (Single Shot MultiBox Detector) are popular for real-time object detection.

3.3 Semantic Segmentation

Semantic segmentation assigns a class label to each pixel in an image, enabling precise object boundaries and understanding of the scene.

Example: Fully Convolutional Networks (FCNs) and U-Net are commonly used for semantic segmentation tasks in medical imaging and autonomous driving.

3.4 Image Generation

CNNs are employed to generate new images based on learned features, such as creating realistic images from noise or generating artworks.

Example: Generative Adversarial Networks (GANs) use CNNs to generate images and have applications in creating art, enhancing resolution, and more.

3.5 Style Transfer

Style transfer involves modifying an image to adopt the style of another image while preserving its content. CNNs are used to extract and blend styles from different images.

Example: Neural Style Transfer algorithms use CNNs to apply artistic styles to photographs, producing images that combine content and artistic elements.

Summary

Deep learning, with its powerful neural network architectures, has transformed many aspects of data science and machine learning. Understanding the architecture of neural networks, including their layers, activation functions, and training processes, provides a solid foundation for applying these models effectively.

Convolutional Neural Networks (CNNs), with their specialized components and applications, are particularly adept at handling spatial data such as images, offering advancements in classification, detection, segmentation, and generation tasks.

By mastering these concepts, data scientists and machine learning practitioners can leverage deep learning techniques to address complex challenges, drive innovation, and achieve high performance in various domains.

Advanced Data Science

Concepts: Natural Language Processing (NLP)

Introduction

Natural Language Processing (NLP) is a field of artificial intelligence that focuses on the interaction between computers and human language. It encompasses a range of techniques to understand, interpret, and generate human language in a way that is both meaningful and useful. This guide covers two significant aspects of NLP: **text processing and sentiment analysis** and the **concept of transformers and attention mechanisms**.

---

1. Text Processing and Sentiment Analysis

Text Processing is the foundational step in NLP that involves converting raw text into a structured format suitable for analysis. **Sentiment Analysis** is a specific application of text processing used to determine the emotional tone behind a series of words.

1.1 Text Processing

Text processing involves several key steps:

1.1.1 Tokenization

Tokenization is the process of splitting text into individual words or tokens. It is a fundamental step in NLP that prepares the text for further analysis.

- **Word Tokenization:** Splits text into words. **Example:** "The quick brown fox" becomes ["The", "quick", "brown", "fox"].

- **Sentence Tokenization:** Splits text into sentences. **Example:** "Hello world. How are you?" becomes ["Hello world.", "How are you?"].

1.1.2 Stop Words Removal

Stop words are common words (such as "and", "the", "is") that are often removed from text during processing as they do not contribute significant meaning.

- **Purpose:** Reduces dimensionality and noise in the text.

- **Example:** "The cat is on the mat" becomes ["cat", "mat"] after removing stop words.

1.1.3 Stemming and Lemmatization

Both stemming and lemmatization are techniques to reduce words to their root forms.

- **Stemming**: Cuts off prefixes or suffixes from words. **Example**: "running", "runner", and "runs" are reduced to "run".

- **Lemmatization**: Reduces words to their base or dictionary form using lexical knowledge. **Example**: "better" is lemmatized to "good".

1.1.4 Part-of-Speech (POS) Tagging

POS tagging involves labeling each word in a sentence with its grammatical role (e.g., noun, verb, adjective).

- **Example**: "The quick brown fox" is tagged as [("The", "DT"), ("quick", "JJ"), ("brown", "JJ"), ("fox", "NN")].

- **Use**: Helps in understanding the syntactic structure and meaning of the text.

1.1.5 Named Entity Recognition (NER)

NER is the process of identifying and classifying named entities in text into predefined categories such as persons, organizations, locations, and dates.

- **Example**: In "Apple Inc. was founded in Cupertino", NER identifies "Apple Inc." as an organization and "Cupertino" as a location.

1.1.6 Text Normalization

Text normalization involves converting text to a standard format, including:

- **Lowercasing**: Converting all characters to lowercase.

- **Removing Punctuation**: Eliminating punctuation marks.

- **Expanding Contractions**: Expanding contractions to their full forms (e.g., "don't" to "do not").

1.1.7 Vectorization

Vectorization transforms text into numerical representations that can be used by machine learning models. Common techniques include:

- **Bag-of-Words (BoW)**: Represents text as a vector of word frequencies.
- **Term Frequency-Inverse Document Frequency (TF-IDF)**: Adjusts word frequencies based on their importance in a document relative to the entire corpus.
- **Word Embeddings**: Uses dense vector representations for words, capturing semantic meaning (e.g., Word2Vec, GloVe).

1.2 Sentiment Analysis

Sentiment Analysis involves determining the sentiment or emotional tone behind a piece of text. It is commonly used to gauge opinions, reviews, and feedback.

1.2.1 Approaches to Sentiment Analysis

- **Lexicon-Based Methods**: Use predefined lists of words with associated sentiment scores to analyze text. **Example**: "happy" might have a positive score, while "sad" has a negative score.
- **Machine Learning-Based Methods**: Train models on labeled datasets to classify text into sentiment categories. **Example**: Sentiment classification into positive, negative, or neutral.

1.2.2 Sentiment Analysis Techniques

- **Rule-Based Systems**: Apply rules and patterns to detect sentiment. **Example**: Sentences with words like "love" or "excellent" are classified as positive.
- **Supervised Learning**: Train models using labeled data (e.g., logistic regression, support vector machines). **Example**: A model trained on movie reviews to predict sentiment.
- **Deep Learning**: Utilize neural networks for more nuanced sentiment analysis. **Example**: Recurrent Neural Networks (RNNs) and Long Short-Term Memory (LSTM) networks for capturing context and dependencies in text.

1.2.3 Applications of Sentiment Analysis

- **Social Media Monitoring**: Analyzing tweets, posts, and comments to gauge public sentiment.
- **Customer Feedback**: Assessing reviews and feedback to improve products and services.
- **Market Research**: Understanding consumer opinions and trends.

---

2. Transformers and Attention Mechanisms

Transformers have become a fundamental architecture in NLP, particularly with their ability to handle long-range dependencies and parallelize processing. The core innovation of transformers is the **attention mechanism**, which allows models to weigh the importance of different parts of the input sequence dynamically.

2.1 The Transformer Architecture

2.1.1 Overview

The Transformer model, introduced by Vaswani et al. in 2017, revolutionized NLP by replacing traditional recurrent neural networks with self-attention mechanisms. It consists of an encoder and a decoder.

Key Components:

- **Encoder**: Processes input sequences and creates representations.
- **Decoder**: Generates output sequences based on encoder representations.

2.1.2 Encoder Layer

The encoder layer has two primary components:

- **Self-Attention Mechanism**: Allows each position in the input sequence to focus on different parts of the sequence.
- **Feed-Forward Neural Network**: Processes the output of the self-attention mechanism.

Each encoder layer consists of:

1. **Self-Attention Mechanism**: Computes attention scores for each token in the sequence with every other token.
2. **Add & Norm**: Applies layer normalization and adds residual connections to the attention output.
3. **Feed-Forward Network**: Applies a feed-forward neural network to each position independently.
4. **Add & Norm**: Applies layer normalization and adds residual connections to the output of the feed-forward network.

2.1.3 Decoder Layer

The decoder layer generates the output sequence and has additional components:

- **Masked Self-Attention Mechanism**: Prevents attending to future tokens in the output sequence.
- **Encoder-Decoder Attention**: Allows the decoder to attend to the encoder's output.
- **Feed-Forward Neural Network**: Similar to the encoder, processes the attention outputs.

Each decoder layer consists of:

1. **Masked Self-Attention Mechanism**: Ensures that the prediction for a position depends only on earlier positions in the sequence.
2. **Add & Norm**: Applies layer normalization and adds residual connections to the masked self-attention output.
3. **Encoder-Decoder Attention**: Attends to the encoder's output using the encoder-decoder attention mechanism.
4. **Add & Norm**: Applies layer normalization and adds residual connections to the encoder-decoder attention output.
5. **Feed-Forward Network**: Applies a feed-forward neural network to each position independently.
6. **Add & Norm**: Applies layer normalization and adds residual connections to the output of the feed-forward network.

2.1.4 Multi-Head Attention

Multi-Head Attention allows the model to focus on different parts of the input sequence simultaneously.

- **Process**: The input is projected into multiple attention heads, each with different parameter sets. The outputs of these heads are concatenated and linearly transformed.
- **Advantage**: Captures various types of relationships and dependencies in the data.

2.1.5 Positional Encoding

Since transformers do not inherently capture the order of tokens, positional encoding is added to provide information about token positions.

- **Formula**:
$$PE(pos, 2i) = \sin\left(\frac{pos}{10000^{2i/d}}\right)$$
$$PE(pos, 2i+1) = \cos\left(\frac{pos}{10000^{2i/d}}\right)$$

where **pos** is the position and i is the dimension.

2.2 Attention Mechanisms

2.2.1 Self-Attention

Self-Attention computes the attention scores within a single sequence, allowing each token to attend to every other token.

Mechanism:

1. **Query, Key, and Value Vectors:** For each token, compute the Query (Q), Key (K), and Value (V) vectors.

2. **Attention Scores:** Compute the attention scores as a dot product of Query and Key vectors, scaled by the square root of the dimension.
   $$\text{Attention Score} = \frac{Q \cdot K^T}{\sqrt{d_k}}$$
   where d_k is the dimension of the Key vectors.

3. **Softmax:** Apply the softmax function to the attention scores to get weights.

4. **Weighted Sum:** Compute the weighted sum of the Value vectors using the attention weights.

2.2.2 Scaled Dot-Product Attention

Scaled Dot-Product Attention improves the performance of self-attention by scaling the dot product of Query and Key vectors.

Steps:

1. **Compute Dot Product:** Calculate the dot product of Query and Key vectors.

2. **Scale:** Divide by the square root of the dimension of the Key vectors.

3. **Softmax:** Apply softmax to obtain attention weights.

4. **Multiply:** Multiply the attention weights by the Value vectors to get the output.

2.2.3 Multi-Head Attention

Multi-Head Attention allows the model to capture multiple types of relationships by performing self-attention multiple times in parallel.

Steps:

1. **Projection:** Project the input into multiple Query, Key, and Value matrices.
2. **Attention Computation:** Perform scaled dot-product attention in parallel for each head.
3. **Concatenate:** Concatenate the outputs of all attention heads.
4. **Linear Transformation:** Apply a linear transformation to the concatenated output.

2.2.4 Applications of Attention Mechanisms

- **Translation:** Used in models like BERT and GPT for translating text from one language to another.
- **Text Summarization:** Helps in summarizing long documents by focusing on important parts.
- **Question Answering:** Improves the accuracy of models that answer questions based on context.

Summary

Natural Language Processing (NLP) and deep learning techniques such as transformers and attention mechanisms have significantly advanced the field of artificial intelligence.

- **Text Processing** involves essential steps like tokenization, stop word removal, stemming, and lemmatization, which prepare raw text for analysis.

- ***Sentiment Analysis*** uses techniques to determine the emotional tone of text, with applications in social media monitoring, customer feedback, and market research.

- ***Transformers*** represent a breakthrough in NLP, with their architecture enabling the effective handling of long-range dependencies and parallel processing. The self-attention mechanism, including multi-head attention, allows transformers to dynamically focus on different parts of the input data.

Understanding these concepts and techniques equips data scientists and machine learning practitioners with the tools to build advanced NLP models, analyze textual data, and address complex language-related tasks effectively.

Advanced Data Science Concepts: AI Ethics

Introduction

As artificial intelligence (AI) systems become increasingly integrated into various aspects of our lives, ethical considerations have become paramount. AI ethics involves examining and addressing the moral implications of AI technologies, including data privacy, bias, and fairness. This guide will explore key ethical considerations in AI and data privacy, as well as discuss bias and fairness in machine learning models.

1. Ethical Considerations in AI and Data Privacy

1.1 Data Privacy

Data privacy is a critical aspect of AI ethics, as AI systems often rely on large datasets that may include sensitive personal information.

1.1.1 Importance of Data Privacy

- ***Personal Information:*** *AI systems frequently process data such as names, addresses, health records, and financial information. Ensuring the privacy of this data is essential to protect individuals' rights and prevent misuse.*
- ***Regulations:*** *Many jurisdictions have established data protection laws to safeguard personal data, such as the General Data Protection Regulation (GDPR) in the European Union and the California Consumer Privacy Act (CCPA) in the United States.*

1.1.2 Data Collection and Consent

- ***Informed Consent:*** *Individuals should be aware of and agree to the collection and use of their data. Consent should be obtained in a clear and transparent manner.*
- ***Purpose Limitation:*** *Data should be collected only for specific, legitimate purposes and not be used for unrelated activities.*

1.1.3 Data Minimization and Security

- ***Data Minimization:*** *Collect only the data necessary for the intended purpose. Avoid excessive data collection that may increase the risk of privacy breaches.*
- ***Data Security:*** *Implement robust security measures to protect data from unauthorized access, breaches, or leaks. This includes encryption, access controls, and regular security audits.*

1.1.4 Data Anonymization and De-Identification

- **Anonymization**: Process of removing personally identifiable information from data sets, so individuals cannot be easily identified.
- **De-Identification**: Involves removing or altering personal identifiers in data to reduce the risk of identification while retaining the data's usability.

1.1.5 Rights and Access

- **Right to Access**: Individuals should have the right to access their data and obtain information on how it is used.
- **Right to Erasure**: Also known as the "right to be forgotten," individuals can request the deletion of their data when it is no longer needed or if they withdraw consent.

---

2. Bias and Fairness in Machine Learning Models

2.1 Understanding Bias

Bias in machine learning models can lead to unfair treatment of individuals or groups and can stem from various sources.

2.1.1 Sources of Bias

- **Data Bias**: Biases present in the training data can propagate into the model. For example, if the data is not representative of the population, the model's predictions will be skewed. **Example**: If a facial recognition system is trained predominantly on images of light-skinned individuals, it may perform poorly on people with darker skin tones.

- ***Algorithmic Bias:*** *Bias introduced through the design of algorithms or their implementation. Some algorithms may amplify existing biases in the data. **Example:** A recommendation system that perpetuates stereotypes based on user behavior patterns.*
- ***Human Bias:*** *Bias introduced by the developers' subjective decisions and assumptions during the design and training of the model.*

2.1.2 Types of Bias

- ***Prejudice Bias:*** *Arises from historical or societal inequalities reflected in the training data.*
- ***Measurement Bias:*** *Results from inaccuracies in the data collection process.*
- ***Selection Bias:*** *Occurs when certain groups or individuals are underrepresented in the dataset.*

2.2 Addressing Bias and Ensuring Fairness

Ensuring fairness in machine learning models involves identifying, mitigating, and monitoring biases throughout the development lifecycle.

2.2.1 Fairness Definitions

- ***Disparate Impact:*** *Occurs when a model's decisions disproportionately affect certain groups compared to others.*
- ***Disparate Treatment:*** *Occurs when individuals are treated differently based on protected attributes such as race, gender, or age.*

2.2.2 Techniques for Mitigating Bias

- **Data Collection:** Ensure the dataset is representative and includes diverse examples. Actively seek to identify and correct imbalances in the data.

- **Bias Detection:** Use statistical tests and metrics to detect biases in the model's predictions. **Example:** Fairness metrics such as demographic parity or equalized odds can help assess whether different groups are treated equitably.

- **Algorithmic Adjustments:** Modify algorithms to reduce bias. Techniques include reweighting samples, using fairness constraints, and incorporating fairness-aware algorithms. **Example:** Implementing fairness constraints during model training to ensure that the model's performance is balanced across different demographic groups.

- **Transparency and Accountability:** Increase transparency by documenting and disclosing the model's design, data sources, and decision-making processes. Establish accountability mechanisms to address and rectify any issues that arise. **Example:** Conducting external audits of AI systems to evaluate their fairness and ethical implications.

2.2.3 Continuous Monitoring and Evaluation

- **Performance Monitoring:** Regularly evaluate the model's performance to ensure it remains fair and unbiased over time.

- **Feedback Loops:** Incorporate feedback from affected individuals and communities to identify and address potential biases.

3. Case Studies and Real-World Applications

3.1 Case Study: Facial Recognition Technology

Issue: Numerous studies have highlighted biases in facial recognition systems, including higher error rates for individuals with darker skin tones and women.

Solution: Researchers and companies have worked to improve fairness by:

- **Diversifying Training Data:** Including more diverse and representative samples in training datasets.
- **Algorithmic Adjustments:** Implementing fairness-aware algorithms to reduce disparity in error rates.

3.2 Case Study: Hiring Algorithms

Issue: AI-driven hiring tools have faced criticism for perpetuating biases based on gender, race, and age.

Solution: Organizations have taken steps to:

- **Audit and Validate:** Regularly audit hiring algorithms for fairness and adjust them based on findings.
- **Transparent Practices:** Ensure transparency in the algorithm's decision-making criteria and involve diverse teams in the development process.

3.3 Case Study: Predictive Policing

Issue: Predictive policing systems have been criticized for reinforcing existing biases in the criminal justice system, leading to disproportionate targeting of minority communities.

Solution: Efforts to address these issues include:

- **Reevaluating Algorithms**: Revising predictive models to consider the broader social context and reduce reliance on biased historical data.
- **Engaging Communities**: Involving community stakeholders in discussions about the ethical implications of predictive policing.

Summary

AI ethics encompasses a range of critical considerations, including data privacy and fairness. Ensuring that AI systems uphold ethical standards involves:

- **Data Privacy**: Safeguarding personal information, obtaining informed consent, and implementing robust security measures.
- **Bias and Fairness**: Identifying and mitigating biases in machine learning models, ensuring fairness across different demographic groups, and continuously monitoring and evaluating the models.

Addressing these ethical challenges is essential for developing AI technologies that are both effective and equitable. By adhering to ethical principles and implementing best practices, organizations can build trust with users, promote transparency, and contribute to the responsible advancement of AI.

Comprehensive Guide to Mock Interviews for Data Science: Practice, Feedback, and Tips

Introduction

Preparing for a data science interview involves not only understanding theoretical concepts and technical skills but also honing the ability to effectively communicate your knowledge and problem-solving process. This guide provides a detailed approach to conducting mock interviews for data science positions, including common questions, practice scenarios, and feedback mechanisms to improve performance.

---

1. Mock Interview Structure

1.1 Interview Format

Mock interviews should simulate real interview conditions to help candidates prepare effectively. A typical data science interview might include:

- **Introduction (5-10 minutes)**: Brief introduction, background, and career goals.
- **Technical Questions (20-30 minutes)**: Questions on data science concepts, algorithms, and problem-solving.
- **Case Study or Problem-Solving (30-40 minutes)**: Practical scenarios or coding problems.
- **Behavioral Questions (10-15 minutes)**: Questions on teamwork, challenges, and conflict resolution.
- **Q&A and Wrap-Up (5-10 minutes)**: Opportunity for the candidate to ask questions and discuss next steps.

2. Common Data Science Questions and Practice Scenarios

2.1 Technical Questions

2.1.1 Statistics and Probability

Question 1: Explain the difference between mean, median, and mode. Provide examples where each measure would be used.

Answer:

- **Mean:** The average of a dataset, calculated by summing all values and dividing by the number of values. Example: For the dataset [3, 5, 7], the mean is (3+5+7)/3 = 5.

- **Median:** The middle value in a sorted dataset. If the number of values is even, it's the average of the two middle values. Example: For [1, 3, 5], the median is 3. For [1, 2, 3, 4], the median is (2+3)/2 = 2.5.

- **Mode:** The value that appears most frequently in a dataset. Example: For [1, 2, 2, 3, 4], the mode is 2.

Question 2: What are probability distributions? Explain normal and binomial distributions.

Answer:

- **Probability Distributions:** Functions that describe the likelihood of different outcomes in a random experiment.

- **Normal Distribution:** Symmetrical, bell-shaped distribution where most of the data falls near the mean. Characterized by mean (μ) and standard deviation (σ). Example: Heights of people in a population often follow a normal distribution.

- **Binomial Distribution:** Represents the number of successes in a fixed number of independent Bernoulli trials with the same probability of success. Example: Flipping a coin 10 times and counting the number of heads.

2.1.2 Data Cleaning

Question 1: How would you handle missing data in a dataset?

Answer:

- **Deletion:** Remove rows or columns with missing values if they constitute a small portion of the data.
- **Imputation:** Fill missing values with a statistical measure (mean, median, mode) or use predictive models. Example: Imputing missing values in a numerical column with the mean of that column.
- **Flagging:** Create a new feature to indicate whether data was missing.

Question 2: Explain how you would detect and handle outliers in a dataset.

Answer:

- **Detection:** Use methods like Z-scores, IQR (Interquartile Range), or visualization (box plots). Example: An outlier is a value that lies beyond 1.5 times the IQR above the third quartile or below the first quartile.

- **Handling**: Depending on context, outliers can be removed, capped, or treated separately. Example: Removing outliers from a dataset to prevent skewing results.

2.1.3 Machine Learning

Question 1: Explain the difference between supervised and unsupervised learning.

Answer:

- **Supervised Learning**: Uses labeled data to train models, where the output is known. Example: Predicting house prices using historical data with features like size and location.
- **Unsupervised Learning**: Uses unlabeled data to identify patterns or groupings. Example: Clustering customers based on purchasing behavior without pre-defined labels.

Question 2: What is overfitting and underfitting? How can you address these issues?

Answer:

- **Overfitting**: When a model learns the training data too well, capturing noise and leading to poor generalization on new data. Solution: Use techniques like cross-validation, regularization, and pruning.
- **Underfitting**: When a model is too simple to capture the underlying patterns in the data. Solution: Use more complex models, add features, or reduce regularization.

2.1.4 Advanced Algorithms

Question 1: Describe how decision trees work.

Answer:

- ***Decision Trees:*** *Models that split data into subsets based on feature values, creating a tree-like structure of decisions.*
- ***Process:*** *Start at the root node and make splits based on feature values to partition the data, aiming to increase purity in each leaf node. Example: A decision tree for classifying animals might split based on attributes like "has feathers" and "can fly."*

Question 2: Explain k-nearest neighbors (k-NN) algorithm.

Answer:

- ***k-NN:*** *A non-parametric, instance-based learning algorithm used for classification and regression.*
- ***Process:*** *For a new instance, find the k nearest neighbors in the training set based on distance metrics (e.g., Euclidean distance). Assign the class or value based on the majority vote or average of these neighbors. Example: Classifying a new point based on the majority class of its k closest neighbors.*

2.1.5 Model Evaluation

Question 1: What are cross-validation techniques, and why are they important?

Answer:

- ***Cross-Validation:*** *A technique to assess the model's performance by partitioning data into training and validation sets multiple times.*

- **Process**: Common methods include k-fold cross-validation, where data is divided into k subsets, and each subset is used once as a validation set while the remaining k-1 subsets are used for training. Importance: Provides a more reliable estimate of model performance and helps in identifying overfitting.

Question 2: Explain precision, recall, and F1-score.

Answer:

- **Precision**: The ratio of true positive predictions to the total number of positive predictions (true positives + false positives).
$$\text{Precision} = \frac{TP}{TP + FP}$$

- **Recall**: The ratio of true positive predictions to the total number of actual positives (true positives + false negatives).
$$\text{Recall} = \frac{TP}{TP + FN}$$

- **F1-Score**: The harmonic mean of precision and recall, providing a single metric to evaluate performance.
$$\text{F1-Score} = 2 \times \frac{\text{Precision} \times \text{Recall}}{\text{Precision} + \text{Recall}}$$

2.1.6 Feature Engineering

Question 1: Discuss feature scaling and normalization.

Answer:

- **Feature Scaling**: Adjusting features to a common scale to improve model performance.

- **Standardization**: Scaling features to have zero mean and unit variance.
  $$\text{Standardized} = \frac{x - \mu}{\sigma}$$

- **Min-Max Scaling**: Rescaling features to a fixed range, usually [0, 1].
  $$\text{Scaled} = \frac{x - \text{min}}{\text{max} - \text{min}}$$

- **Normalization**: Adjusting features to ensure they have the same scale, which is especially important for algorithms sensitive to feature magnitudes.

Question 2: Explain dimensionality reduction techniques, such as Principal Component Analysis (PCA).

Answer:

- **PCA**: A technique to reduce the number of features by transforming the data into a set of orthogonal components that capture the most variance.

- **Process**: Compute the eigenvectors and eigenvalues of the covariance matrix to determine principal components. Project the data onto these components to reduce dimensionality while preserving important variance.

---

3. Behavioral Questions

3.1 Common Behavioral Questions

Question 1: Describe a challenging project you worked on and how you overcame obstacles.

Answer:

- **Example Response**: Discuss a project where you faced significant challenges, such as data quality issues or tight deadlines. Explain the steps you took to overcome these challenges, such as improving data cleaning processes, collaborating with team members, or managing your time effectively.

Question 2: How do you handle disagreements or conflicts within a team?

Answer:

- **Example Response**: Discuss your approach to resolving conflicts, such as listening to different perspectives, finding common ground, and facilitating open communication. Provide an example where you successfully resolved a conflict and achieved a positive outcome.

3.2 Tips for Answering Behavioral Questions

- **Use the STAR Method**: Structure your responses using Situation, Task, Action, and Result.

- **Be Specific**: Provide concrete examples and details to illustrate your experiences.

- **Highlight Key Skills**: Emphasize relevant skills such as problem-solving, teamwork, and communication.

---

4. Practice Scenarios and Coding Problems

4.1 Practice Scenarios

Scenario 1: You have a dataset with multiple features, including some categorical and some numerical. Your task is to build a predictive model. Describe your approach to preprocessing and feature engineering.

Example Response:

- **Data Preprocessing**: Handle missing values, encode categorical features (e.g., one-hot encoding), and normalize numerical features.
- **Feature Engineering**: Create new features based on existing ones, such as interaction terms or aggregated statistics.

Scenario 2: A company wants to implement a recommendation system for its e-commerce platform. How would you design this system, and what algorithms might you use?

Example Response:

- **Design**: Use collaborative filtering to recommend products based on user preferences and behavior. Combine with content-based filtering to recommend similar products based on product features.
- **Algorithms**: Implement matrix factorization techniques (e.g., Singular Value Decomposition) and nearest neighbors algorithms.

4.2 Coding Problems

Problem 1: Write a function to perform k-means clustering on a given dataset. The function should return the cluster centers and labels for each data point.

Example Solution:

python

Code

```python
import numpy as np
from sklearn.cluster import KMeans

def perform_kmeans(data, n_clusters):
    kmeans = KMeans(n_clusters=n_clusters, random_state=0).fit(data)
    return kmeans.cluster_centers_, kmeans.labels_
```

Problem 2: Implement a function to evaluate the performance of a classification model using confusion matrix metrics (precision, recall, F1-score).

Example Solution:

python

Code

```python
from sklearn.metrics import precision_score, recall_score, f1_score

def evaluate_classification_model(y_true, y_pred):
    precision = precision_score(y_true, y_pred)
    recall = recall_score(y_true, y_pred)
    f1 = f1_score(y_true, y_pred)
    return precision, recall, f1
```

5. Feedback and Tips for Improvement

5.1 Providing Feedback

5.1.1 Technical Accuracy

- **Check Knowledge**: Ensure the candidate demonstrates a strong understanding of technical concepts.
- **Correct Mistakes**: Point out any errors in their explanations or coding solutions and provide the correct information.

5.1.2 Problem-Solving Approach

- **Evaluate Process**: Assess how the candidate approaches problems, including their problem-solving strategy and coding practices.
- **Suggest Improvements**: Provide feedback on how they can improve their approach or coding practices.

5.1.3 Communication Skills

- **Clarity**: Ensure the candidate explains their answers clearly and concisely.
- **Structure**: Encourage the use of structured responses, such as the STAR method for behavioral questions.

5.2 Tips for Improvement

5.2.1 Technical Skills

- **Practice Coding**: Regularly solve coding problems on platforms like LeetCode or HackerRank.
- **Review Concepts**: Revisit key data science concepts and algorithms to strengthen your understanding.

5.2.2 Problem-Solving

- **Work on Projects**: Apply your knowledge to real-world projects to gain practical experience.

- **Collaborate:** Work with peers or mentors to discuss and solve problems.

5.2.3 Communication

- **Mock Interviews:** Participate in mock interviews to practice articulating your thoughts and answers.
- **Seek Feedback:** Request feedback from peers or mentors on your interview performance and areas for improvement.

Conclusion

Preparing for data science interviews requires a blend of technical knowledge, problem-solving skills, and effective communication. Conducting mock interviews with common questions, practice scenarios, and coding problems is essential for honing these skills. By actively seeking feedback and implementing improvement strategies, candidates can enhance their interview performance and increase their chances of success in securing a data science role.

Conclusion: Khamoshi: Echoes of Silence

In the tapestry of life, some stories are woven with threads of professional ambition, personal connection, and profound growth. "Khamoshi: Echoes of Silence" is one such narrative that intricately blends these elements into a compelling tale of love and learning. This concluding chapter seeks to reflect on the journey of Aditi and Arjun, exploring how their shared passions and enduring commitment shaped their relationship and professional achievements.

---

1. The Interplay of Professional and Personal Growth

1.1 Shared Passions as a Foundation

Aditi and Arjun's journey begins at the intersection of their professional lives. Both are dedicated AI researchers with a deep passion for data science. Their initial connection, forged through a data science conference, sets the stage for a collaboration that transcends mere professional interaction. This shared interest in AI becomes the foundation of their relationship.

- ***Common Ground***: Their mutual enthusiasm for data science creates a strong bond, allowing them to connect on a deeper level. This professional alignment not only fosters respect but also cultivates a sense of partnership.

- ***Intellectual Chemistry***: The ability to discuss complex data science topics with someone who understands and shares the same passion strengthens their connection. This intellectual synergy plays a crucial role in deepening their personal relationship.

1.2 Navigating Challenges Together

As their relationship evolves, Aditi and Arjun face significant challenges, including misunderstandings and periods of silence. These obstacles test their bond and communication skills.

- ***Misunderstandings***: The initial misunderstanding regarding their project deadlines creates a rift between them. This period of silence underscores the importance of clear communication and the impact of unresolved conflicts on personal and professional relationships.

- ***Silence and Reflection***: The two-week period of silence is a crucial phase in their journey. It forces both Aditi and Arjun to reflect on their feelings, reassess their priorities, and understand the value of their relationship.

1.3 Reconnecting and Growing Together

The resolution of their silence marks a turning point in their relationship. This period of introspection leads to a deeper understanding of each other's needs and aspirations.

- **Open Communication:** The conversation that follows their period of silence is transformative. It provides an opportunity to address past issues, express their feelings, and discuss their future together.

- **Personal Growth:** The challenges they face together, including their commitment to learning and professional development, contribute to their personal growth. This growth is not just limited to their careers but extends to their relationship.

---

2. The Journey of Learning and Love

2.1 Embracing Continuous Learning

Aditi and Arjun's commitment to continuous learning becomes a defining aspect of their relationship. Over the course of 75 days, they engage in a structured learning journey that blends romance with education.

- **Daily Learning:** Their daily interactions revolve around various data science topics, from the basics of statistics and probability to advanced machine learning algorithms and AI ethics. This structured approach not only enhances their professional skills but also strengthens their bond.

- **Romantic Touches:** Incorporating unique, romantic gestures into their learning sessions adds a personal touch to their professional growth. This creative approach fosters a sense of intimacy and reinforces their commitment to each other.

2.2 Overcoming Challenges Through Learning

The process of preparing for interviews and solving complex problems together serves as a testament to their teamwork and resilience.

- **Collaborative Effort**: Working on data science problems and mock interviews together allows them to leverage each other's strengths and overcome challenges. This collaborative effort enhances their problem-solving skills and builds a deeper understanding of each other's capabilities.

- **Celebrating Success**: Their successful interview preparation and job placements are celebrated as milestones in their journey. This success not only validates their hard work but also symbolizes the strength of their partnership.

3. Reflections on Silence and Communication

3.1 The Role of Silence

The concept of "Khamoshi" or silence plays a significant role in Aditi and Arjun's journey. It serves as a period of reflection and growth.

- **Silence as a Teacher**: The silence between Aditi and Arjun is not merely a pause but a time for introspection and personal growth. It teaches them about the importance of communication and understanding in a relationship.

- **Renewed Connection**: Breaking the silence leads to a renewed connection, where they are able to address past issues and express their commitment to each other.

3.2 The Power of Communication

Effective communication emerges as a cornerstone of their relationship. The ability to discuss their challenges, express their feelings, and plan their future together strengthens their bond.

- **Open Dialogue:** The deep conversations that follow their silence help clarify misunderstandings and align their goals. This open dialogue is crucial for building a strong and lasting relationship.

- **Shared Dreams:** Communicating their shared dreams and aspirations allows them to build a future together, blending their personal and professional goals.

---

4. The Enduring Bond

4.1 Celebrating Achievements

The culmination of Aditi and Arjun's journey is marked by their professional achievements and personal growth. Their success in securing positions as AI researchers is a testament to their dedication and teamwork.

- **Professional Success:** Their successful interviews and job placements reflect their commitment to continuous learning and collaboration. This success is not only a career milestone but also a celebration of their partnership.

- **Personal Fulfillment:** Their journey is a celebration of their personal growth and the strength of their relationship. It highlights how shared passions and mutual support contribute to a fulfilling and enduring partnership.

4.2 Looking Forward

As Aditi and Arjun look to the future, they do so with a sense of accomplishment and optimism. Their journey serves as a reminder of the power of love and learning in shaping a meaningful and enduring relationship.

- **Future Plans**: They envision a future where their personal and professional goals continue to align, and their relationship remains a source of strength and inspiration.

- **Commitment**: Their story underscores the importance of commitment, communication, and shared passions in building a lasting and fulfilling relationship.

Conclusion

"Khamoshi: Echoes of Silence" is more than a narrative of professional and personal growth; it is a testament to the profound impact of love and learning on shaping a meaningful relationship. Aditi and Arjun's journey illustrates how shared passions can form the foundation of a strong bond, and how effective communication can overcome challenges and strengthen connections.

Their story serves as an inspiration for anyone navigating the complexities of relationships and career aspirations. It highlights the importance of embracing both personal and professional growth, and the value of communication and mutual support in building a lasting partnership.

As we reflect on Aditi and Arjun's journey, we are reminded that the echoes of silence are not just pauses *in time but opportunities for growth and understanding. Their story is a celebration of the power of love and learning, and a testament to the enduring strength of a well-nurtured relationship.*

- **Love:** *Central to the narrative, representing the emotional and personal connection between Aditi and Arjun.*

- **Learning:** *Refers to their commitment to continuous education and professional growth, particularly in data science.*

- **Communication:** *Highlights the importance of dialogue in resolving misunderstandings and strengthening their relationship.*

- **Silence:** *Represents the period of reflection and introspection that affects their relationship and personal growth.*

- **Collaboration**: Reflects their joint efforts in both professional projects and personal development.
- **Passion**: Represents their shared enthusiasm for data science and how it drives their connection and growth.
- **Growth**: Denotes their evolution both professionally and personally throughout the story.

Glossary

1. Accuracy: The degree to which a measured value conforms to the actual value. In classification, it is the ratio of correct predictions to total predictions.

2. AdaBoost: Adaptive Boosting, an ensemble learning technique that combines multiple weak classifiers to create a strong classifier by focusing on the errors made by previous classifiers.

3. Algorithm: A step-by-step procedure or formula for solving a problem or performing a computation.

4. Anomaly Detection: The process of identifying data points that significantly deviate from the norm, often used to detect outliers or unusual patterns.

5. API (Application Programming Interface): A set of protocols and tools for building and interacting with software applications, allowing different systems to communicate.

6. AUC (Area Under the Curve): A metric used in classification problems to evaluate the performance of a model, specifically the ROC (Receiver Operating Characteristic) curve.

7. Bagging: Bootstrap Aggregating, an ensemble learning technique that improves the stability and accuracy of machine learning algorithms by combining predictions from multiple models trained on different subsets of the data.

8. Bias: In machine learning, the error introduced by approximating a real-world problem with a simplified model.

9. Bootstrap: A resampling technique that involves randomly sampling with replacement from the data to create multiple datasets for training models.

10. Classifier: A type of machine learning model used to categorize data into different classes or categories.

11. Clustering: An unsupervised learning technique used to group similar data points together based on their features.

12. Confusion Matrix: A table used to evaluate the performance of a classification model by comparing the predicted and actual class labels.

13. Cross-Validation: A technique used to assess the performance of a model by dividing the data into training and validation sets multiple times.

14. Decision Tree: A model that splits data into subsets based on feature values to make predictions or classifications, creating a tree-like structure of decisions.

15. Deep Learning: A subset of machine learning involving neural networks with many layers (deep networks) that learn representations of data through complex architectures.

16. Dimensionality Reduction: Techniques used to reduce the number of features in a dataset while preserving its essential characteristics, often used to simplify models and improve performance.

17. Ensemble Learning: Combining multiple models to improve overall performance and robustness compared to individual models.

18. Feature Engineering: The process of creating new features or modifying existing features to improve the performance of machine learning models.

19. Feature Scaling: Techniques such as normalization or standardization used to adjust the range or distribution of feature values to improve model performance.

20. F1-Score: A metric that combines precision and recall into a single measure, representing the harmonic mean of these two values.

21. Gradient Descent: An optimization algorithm used to minimize the cost function in machine learning models by iteratively adjusting the model parameters.

22. Hyperparameter: Parameters that are set before the training process begins, influencing the behavior and performance of the machine learning model.

23. Imputation: The process of filling in missing values in a dataset using statistical methods or predictive models.

24. k-Nearest Neighbors (k-NN): A classification algorithm that assigns a class to a data point based on the majority class of its k nearest neighbors in the feature space.

25. Logistic Regression: A statistical model used for binary classification that estimates the probability of a class using a logistic function.

26. Mean Absolute Error (MAE): A regression metric that measures the average magnitude of errors in predictions, without considering their direction.

27. Mean Squared Error (MSE): A regression metric that measures the average squared difference between predicted and actual values.

28. Model Overfitting: When a model learns the training data too well, including noise and outliers, leading to poor generalization on new data.

29. Model Underfitting: When a model is too simple to capture the underlying patterns in the data, resulting in poor performance on both training and validation data.

30. Natural Language Processing (NLP): A field of AI focused on the interaction between computers and human language, including tasks such as text analysis, language generation, and sentiment analysis.

31. Neural Network: A machine learning model inspired by the human brain, consisting of interconnected nodes (neurons) organized in layers.

32. Normalization: The process of scaling features to a standard range, typically [0, 1], to ensure that all features contribute equally to model training.

33. Outlier: A data point that differs significantly from other observations in a dataset, potentially affecting model performance.

34. Precision: A classification metric that measures the proportion of true positive predictions out of all positive predictions made by the model.

35. Recall: A classification metric that measures the proportion of true positive predictions out of all actual positive instances in the dataset.

36. Regularization: Techniques used to prevent overfitting by adding a penalty for complex models, such as L1 (Lasso) or L2 (Ridge) regularization.

37. ROC Curve (Receiver Operating Characteristic Curve): A graphical representation of a model's performance across different classification thresholds, plotting the true positive rate against the false positive rate.

38. Stochastic Gradient Descent (SGD): A variation of gradient descent that updates model parameters using a single or a small batch of training examples at a time.

39. Supervised Learning: A type of machine learning where the model is trained on labeled data to make predictions or classifications based on input-output pairs.

40. Support Vector Machine (SVM): A classification algorithm that finds the optimal hyperplane that maximizes the margin between different classes.

41. Test Set: A subset of data used to evaluate the performance of a trained model and assess its generalization ability on new, unseen data.

42. Training Set: A subset of data used to train a machine learning model by adjusting its parameters based on the input-output pairs.

43. Variance: The degree to which a model's predictions change when trained on different subsets of the data, indicating its sensitivity to fluctuations in the training set.

44. Validation Set: A subset of data used during model training to tune hyperparameters and evaluate intermediate performance before final testing.

45. Feature Selection: The process of choosing a subset of relevant features for model training to improve performance and reduce complexity.

46. Gradient Boosting: An ensemble learning technique that combines multiple weak learners sequentially, each correcting the errors of the previous one, to create a strong predictive model.

47. Principal Component Analysis (PCA): A dimensionality reduction technique that transforms data into a set of orthogonal components that capture the maximum variance.

48. Recurrent Neural Networks (RNNs): A type of neural network designed for sequential data, where connections between nodes can create cycles, allowing the model to maintain context.

49. Random Forest: An ensemble learning method that combines multiple decision trees to improve classification or regression accuracy by averaging their predictions.

50. Scikit-Learn: A popular Python library for machine learning that provides tools for data preprocessing, model selection, and evaluation.

51. TensorFlow: An open-source machine learning framework developed by Google, used for building and training neural networks and other machine learning models.

52. PyTorch: An open-source machine learning library developed by Facebook, known for its dynamic computational graph and ease of use in developing neural networks.

53. Naive Bayes: A classification algorithm based on Bayes' theorem, assuming independence between features, commonly used for text classification tasks.

54. Ensemble Methods: Techniques that combine multiple models to improve overall performance, including bagging, boosting, and stacking.

55. Time Series Analysis: A method used to analyze data points collected or recorded at specific time intervals, often used for forecasting and trend analysis.

56. Collaborative Filtering: A recommendation system approach that predicts user preferences based on past behavior and interactions with other users.

57. Content-Based Filtering: A recommendation system approach that suggests items similar to those the user has shown interest in, based on item features.

58. Data Wrangling: The process of cleaning, transforming, and organizing raw data into a format suitable for analysis.

59. Feature Importance: A measure of how much a feature contributes to the predictions made by a model, often used in feature selection and model interpretation.

60. Hyperparameter Tuning: The process of selecting the best hyperparameters for a machine learning model to optimize its performance.

61. Logistic Function: A sigmoid function used in logistic regression to model probabilities as outputs, bounded between 0 and 1.

62. Mean Squared Logarithmic Error (MSLE): A regression metric that measures the difference between predicted and actual values on a logarithmic scale, focusing on relative differences.

63. Robustness: The ability of a model to maintain its performance despite variations or noise in the input data.

64. Autoencoder: A type of neural network used for unsupervised learning, typically for dimensionality reduction or feature learning, where the output aims to reconstruct the input.

65. Generative Adversarial Network (GAN): A framework for training models that consists of two neural networks, a generator and a discriminator, that compete to improve each other's performance.

66. Softmax Function: A function used in the output layer of neural networks to convert raw scores (logits) into probabilities for classification tasks.

67. Transfer Learning: A technique where a pre-trained model is fine-tuned on a new, related task, leveraging learned features to improve performance.

68. Regularization Parameter: A hyperparameter that controls the amount of regularization applied to a model, influencing its complexity and generalization ability.

69. ROC-AUC Score: The area under the ROC curve, a metric used to evaluate the performance of a binary classification model, with higher values indicating better performance.

70. Data Augmentation: Techniques used to increase the diversity of training data by applying transformations or variations, often used in image processing.

71. Gradient Boosting Machines (GBM): A family of boosting algorithms, including XGBoost, LightGBM, and CatBoost, known for their performance and efficiency in handling large datasets.

72. k-Fold Cross-Validation: A validation technique where the data is split into k subsets, and the model is trained and evaluated k times, each time using a different subset as the test set.

73. Feature Extraction: The process of transforming raw data into a set of features that can be used for model training, often involving techniques like PCA or text vectorization.

74. Dropout: A regularization technique used in neural networks to prevent overfitting by randomly dropping units (neurons) during training.

75. Batch Normalization: A technique used to normalize the inputs of each layer in a neural network to improve training speed and stability.

76. Clustering Algorithm: A type of algorithm used to group data points into clusters based on similarity, such as k-means or hierarchical clustering.

77. Principal Component Analysis (PCA): A dimensionality reduction technique that transforms data into orthogonal components that capture the maximum variance.

78. Cost Function: A function used to measure the performance of a model by calculating the difference between predicted and actual values, also known as the loss function.

79. Learning Rate: A hyperparameter that controls the size of the steps taken during optimization, affecting how quickly a model learns.

80. Precision-Recall Curve: A plot that shows the trade-off between precision and recall for different thresholds, useful for evaluating classification performance.

81. One-Hot Encoding: A technique for representing categorical variables as binary vectors, where each category is represented by a unique vector with a single '1' and the rest '0's.

82. Data Pipeline: A series of data processing steps, including cleaning, transformation, and modeling, designed to automate the workflow from raw data to actionable insights.

83. Support Vector Machine (SVM): A classification algorithm that finds the optimal hyperplane that separates classes in the feature space with the maximum margin.

84. Cross-Entropy Loss: A loss function used in classification tasks that measures the difference between the predicted probability distribution and the actual class labels.

85. Hyperparameter: A parameter whose value is set before the training process and affects the model's training and performance, such as learning rate or number of layers.

86. Feature Map: In convolutional neural networks (CNNs), a feature map is the output of a convolution operation applied to an input image, representing learned features.

87. Convolution: An operation in neural networks where a filter is applied to input data to detect specific features, such as edges or textures in images.

88. Tuning: The process of adjusting model parameters or hyperparameters to optimize performance.

89. Model Deployment: The process of integrating a trained model into a production environment where it can make predictions on new data.

90. Model Interpretation: Techniques used to understand and explain the decisions made by a machine learning model, such as SHAP or LIME.

91. Neural Network Layers: Different layers in a neural network, including input layers, hidden layers, and output layers, each performing specific functions in data processing.

92. Tokenization: The process of breaking down text into individual tokens or words, often used as a preprocessing step in NLP tasks.

93. Precision-Recall Tradeoff: The balance between precision and recall in classification tasks, where improving one may reduce the other.

94. K-Means Clustering: An unsupervised learning algorithm that partitions data into k clusters by minimizing the variance within each cluster.

95. Data Leakage: The inadvertent introduction of information from outside the training dataset into the model training process, leading to overestimation of model performance.

96. Gradient Boosting: An ensemble technique that builds models sequentially, where each model corrects the errors of its predecessor.

97. Token Embedding: A method of converting tokens into numerical vectors that capture semantic meaning, used in NLP tasks.

98. Backpropagation: An algorithm used to train neural networks by propagating the error gradients backward through the network to update the weights.

99. Learning Curve: A plot that shows the model's performance on training and validation sets over time, helping to diagnose issues like overfitting or underfitting.

100. Data Visualization: The graphical representation of data to uncover patterns, trends, and insights, often using tools like matplotlib or seaborn.

www.ingramcontent.com/pod-product-compliance
Lightning Source LLC
Chambersburg PA
CBHW062102220526
45471CB00010B/3572